# The Gibson "P.A.F." Humbucking Pickup From Myth to Reality

Mario Milan & James Finnerty

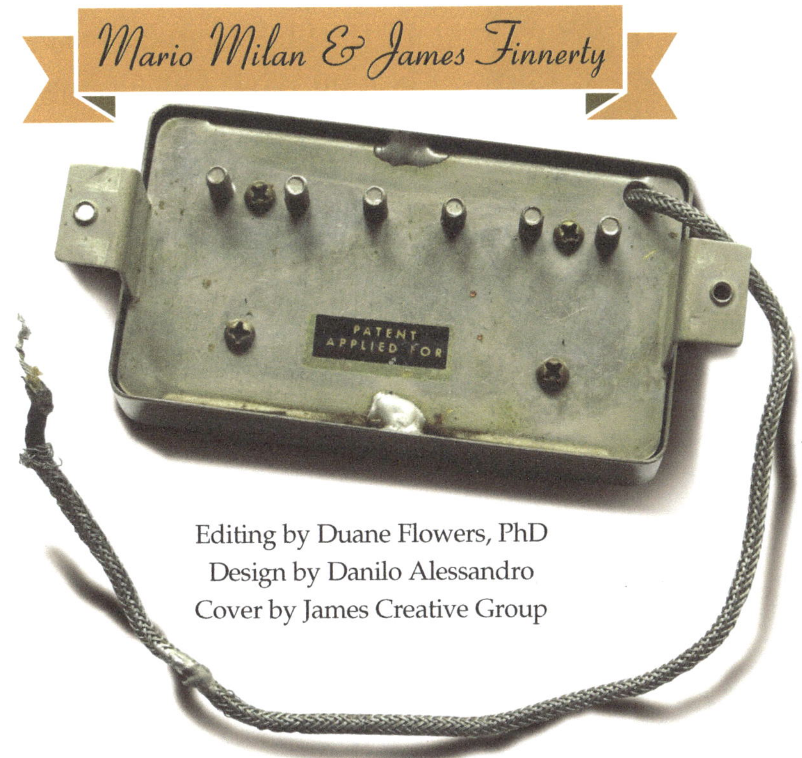


Editing by Duane Flowers, PhD
Design by Danilo Alessandro
Cover by James Creative Group

ISBN: 978-1-57424-364-2
SAN 683-8022

P.O. Box 17878 - Anaheim Hills, CA 92817

www.centerstream-usa.com | centerstrm@aol.com | 714-779-9390

Mario Milan is a guitar player who worked for a while as a composer for the Italian RCA Company, just long enough to realize that they were not interested at all in blues-based music, which was and still remains his main interest.
In 1994 he became a writer for the Italian guitar publication AXE Guitar Magazine, specializing in articles about blues players and vintage guitars. (http://www.axemagazine.it/).
In 2006 he published the book "Windings and Magnets... And the Guitar Became Electric" for Centerstream, about the history of the electric guitar and how pickup designs evolved through the years.

James Finnerty is the founder of the ReWind Electric Company, and is a builder of fine pickups with a good range of humbucking and single coil models patterned after historic Gibson P.A.F. and P 90 original models. His broad knowledge of the technical aspects of pickup building, his desire to share information, and his ability to explain even the most intricate aspects of matters concerning pickups with simplicity, made him an ideal partner for a project on the history and the engineering aspects of the Gibson "Patent Applied For" Pickup. His attention to detail, scientific approach to repair, and study of vintage pickups, allowed him to compile a broad database and to gain an uncommon knowledge of the many variations in magnet formulas and coil geometry on these iconic pickups.

# Acknowledgments

We want to say thank you to:

Jeffrey Allen
Alessandro Angelucci
Vincenzo Atzori
Francesco Balossino
David Bowes (Sigil Pickups)
Claudio Caldana
Fabrizio Dadò (Axe Guitar Magazine)
Stefano Gaibazzi (Re Caster)
Cole Gaskins
Regina Gorham at the Kalamazoo Valley Museum
Carl Grefenstette (owappleton.com)
Jon Gundry (Throbak Electronics)
John Kontos
Lowell Levinger (Players Vintage Instruments)
Jason Lollar (Lollar Guitars)
Wolfe Mcleod (Wolfetone Pickups)
Alex Merrill at the Kalamazoo Public Library
Tim Mills (Bareknuckle Pickups)
Eva Passerini
Furio Pozzi
Claudio Prosperini
Alex Solca
Dave Stephens (Stephens Design)
Mark Stow (Ox4 Pickups)
Fred Stuart
Franco Tonini
Miraldo Vidal
Aleksandar Vrhovec (Wizz Pickups)
Lynn Weelwright

...dedicated to my mother...(Mario Milan)

# Table of contents

# Introduction

*1957 ES 175D (left) and 1962 ES 175DN (right). These two Gibson guitars represent the classic time frame of the "P.A.F." era, even though the humbucking pickup was introduced on some pedal steels in 1956.*

Since the beginning, Gibson has always been innovative, but has always been guided by the principle that any new designs maintain a classic elegance.

The instruments that Orville Gibson was building toward the end of the 19th Century were structurally different from anything else being done at the time. He carved solid woods and arched tops and was inspired by the way violins were traditionally made, while aesthetically recalling finely crafted Renaissance instruments.

When Lloyd A. Loar was later involved in the design of the Master Model line of instruments with the famous L-5, that guitar not only became a standard for its tonal quality, but for its elegance as well, thereby establishing itself as a classic.

At first Gibson was reluctant to add a solid body model to its line of electric guitars, but when they did, again, the result was another classic, with a simple, yet appealing design.

The Les Paul was essentially a scaled down solid archtop and the colors that were chosen (gold for the Standard model, black with gold hardware for the Custom, and limed mahogany or cherry for the lower cost Junior and Special models) seemed to enhance the wholesomeness of the shape.

The evolution of the high-end models saw the introduction of several innovations, such as the Tune-O-Matic Bridge and a series of pickup iterations, which progressed from the original P 90 for the main model and the dual AlNiCo model P 90 for the Custom, to the newly designed humbucking pickups.

Then the Les Paul Model, in 1958, got a new cherry sunburst finish, which revealed the sometimes striking figuring of the Michigan maple used for the tops.

*1915 Gibson Style O, innovation and classic elagance in a single package.*

*1958 Gibson ES 125. The Gibson electric archtop line defined how a "jazz" guitar was supposed to sound.*

New guitars were also added, like the ES 335TD ("TD" for "thin line, double pickup") and was soon followed by the fancier ES 345TD, the ES 355TD-SV, the Explorer, the Flying V (all equipped with humbucking pickups) and the Firebird (with proprietary mini-humbucking pickups).

The original Gibson humbucking pickup, known as the "Patent Applied For" (P.A.F.), later became a collector's item on his own, and the point of reference to which any variant made since is compared.The same principles behind the design of the Gibson humbucking pickup have been used on many models, even when pursuing a completely different type of performance or tonal quality, ranging from the Super Distortion model to the mini-humbucking model used on the Stratocaster.

At the time, Gibson was the leading brand in the industry, with a line of archtop electric guitars that set the standard for any competitor, challenging Martin in the acoustic guitar field and remaining bravely innovative with a growing offering of solid body guitars.

*Gibson "Patent Applied For" Pickups.*

*1957 Gibson Les Paul Special.*

*1961 Gibson Les Paul Standard. A sleek new style for the rock player.*

# The Gibson Factory

*The Gibson Factory, at 225 Parsons Street, Kalamazoo, Michigan. c. 1941*

*1913*
*Gibson Style O.*

In 1897 Orville Gibson made his first impressive instruments in a shop at 114 South Burdick Street, and two years later moved to the second floor of 104 East Main Street, in the center of Kalamazoo, Michigan. Born on a farm near Chateaugay, in upstate New York, Gibson moved to Kalamazoo when he was 25 years old and little is known about how he became interested in lutherie. Walter Carter, in Gibson Guitars: 100 Years of an American Icon (General Pub Group, 1996) wrote: "Kalamazoo. The name rolls off the tongue like some far-off fairytale land". Moreover, the story of Orville Gibson, working as a clerk in a shoe store to finance his vision of becoming the main musical instruments builder in the "Big Village", as Kalamazoo was nicknamed, sounds like a fairytale indeed.

Orville's success as a builder of original and fine instruments did not go unnoticed, and in 1902 a group of investors signed an agreement with him for the production, distribution and sale of instruments of his design. Thus, the Gibson Mandolin-Guitar Manufacturing Co. Ltd. was established. The plant used was an old bakery at 114 East Exchange Place in downtown Kalamazoo. Michigan included woodworking as one of its largest economic assets, so the simple happenstance of being located in Kalamazoo, allowed Gibson to train already experienced woodworkers to become skilled instrument makers.
Among the most iconic instruments introduced were the Style O Guitar, with an elaborate scrolled upper horn, oval hole, and arched top, and the Style U Harp Guitar, with eleven strings added to provide bass accompaniment to the normal six strings.

Very soon they had to expand, and in 1911 they moved to a new, larger place, located at 523 East Harrison Court. In 1915 a new agreement was signed, giving the company the right to design, produce and sell instruments and other products under the Gibson name, while Orville, who at that time had health problems, would receive a lifelong monthly royalty.
Orville Gibson died of endocarditis at St. Lawrence State Hospital in Ogdensburg, New York on August 21, 1918 at the age of 62.

As production continued to increase, the Gibson Company, which by that time was producing a broad range of string instruments including mandolins and banjos, acquired land to build a new factory, which was completed in 1917. This new building was at 225 Parsons Street, and in the following decades, it would become probably the most famous musical instrument manufacturing plant in the industry.

It was here that Lloyd Loar designed the Master Series of instruments, with the L-5 Archtop Guitar, the F-5 Mandolin, and the Mastertone TB-5 Banjo. They later built the electric lap steels and the ES 150 electric guitar here. Some of Gibson's outstanding achievements from that era are the adjustable truss-rod (invented by Ted McHugh), the most dominant archtop line (peaking with the impressive Super 400), and the pedal steel Electraharp (designed with John Moore).

*The Gibson Factory, interior 1936. From the original captions: Cutting Raw Materials, "Woods for instruments come from all over the world: Ebony from Madagascar; Rosewood from Brazil; Mahogany from British Honduras. (top)*
*"...where the binding is glued to the edges of the bodies of the instruments." (bottom)*

*"Several unidentified men at work benches. Many guitar bodies on wheeled racks or hanging from the ceiling." (top)*
*"One section of the general assembling room." (bottom)*

In 1902 13 people were working at the factory, and in 1927 there were 130. During this time the company was being run by its board of managers. World War II forced Gibson to reduce instrument output and cooperate with the army, making parts for machine guns, radar, and other precision items. The job done at Gibson was so good that in recognition the company received three Awards for Excellence in 1944, which was the year it was bought by Chicago Musical Instruments (which, in 1969 was acquired by the Panama-based Ecuadorian Company, Ltd. which was soon renamed to Norlin Corporation).

After the war, Gibson was not healthy financially, but by the end of the forties it was again turning a profit, and in 1955 the Gibson factory was completely reorganized. As reported in Gil Hembree's book Gibson Guitars, Ted McCarty's Golden Era (Hal Leonard, 2007), interviews with Gibson employees revealed that the atmosphere in the factory was that of a family-like environment, albeit with better salaries than other factories in the area. A place where the work was hard, but the employees were proud of that work.

*1924 L-5 guitar, 1924 H-5 Mandola and 1923 F-5 Mandolin.*

Whatever the job, making strings, sanding guitars, shaping necks, they all seemed to deeply believe in what they were doing, which was making musical instruments of a superior nature. Usually, the woodworking was handled by the men, as more physical strength was required and potentially dangerous tools had to be used. String making, electronic assembly and pickup winding were mostly women's jobs. However, there was always some flexibility, if somebody wanted to change jobs, they were always allowed to try. Gibson President Ted McCarty estimated that about 40% of the employees were women, a few of them, in fact, preferring woodworking to making strings or winding pickups.

Since Gibson was expanding, it was not unusual for women to quit their jobs for a while if they had children to raise, and return to work a few years later, even if in the meantime somebody had been hired to fill the vacancy. There was always an ever increasing demand for experienced employees.

McCarty's assistant at this time was John Huis, Superintendent and Vice President in Charge of Production. Clarence Havenga was Vice President and Sales Manager. Musician Wilbur Marker was the Head of Customer Service. Julius Bell- son was Assistant Treasurer. E. P. Morse was Vice President and Legal Counsel. Maurice H. Berlin was Secretary-Treasurer, with Thomas V. Naylor as his Assistant Secretary. The Chief Engineer was Larry Allers, who was responsible for prototypes (he was the main designer of the Les Paul guitar and the Les Paul SG). Rollo Werner was in charge of wood selection and procurement.

The electronics area was led by Walter Fuller, with Seth Lover as his assistant. Walter Fuller was the engineer who designed the bar pickup (which was also known as the "Charlie Christian" pickup), a long diagonal pickup, the metal covered P 13 single coil pickup of 1941, and its successor, the legendary P 90. Seth Lover was hired to work on amplifiers as he had studied radio technology since his teen years. He designed a noise-free choke for the amps and the vibrato circuit for the Les Paul line of amps, which included the GA 20 and GA 40T.

Lover also designed the AlNiCo pickup (also known as the "Staple" pickup), the humbucking pickup, the mini-humbucking pickup for the newly acquired Epiphone guitars (a variant of which was sold to other makers such as Silvertone), and the pickups for the Firebird Series. Later, Lover would be hired by CBS to design pickups for Fender, and the result was the first humbucking model for that brand; a large humbucker with cunife magnets, which was also known as the "Wide Range" Humbucker.

Rem Wall, a fine musician and well-known singer of the time who was also a local TV personality and performed with the band Green Valley Boys, was in charge of the final inspection of any guitar and amp built. He played each and every one of them looking for eventual defects in performance or craftsmanship with the help of a few guys who would file the occasional buzzing fret. They sent any amplifiers with concerns back to the electronics department.

*1962 Gibson Les Paul, with vibrola removed.*

All the instruments not meeting the high standards set by McCarty were rejected, and unfortunately, after he resigned, such strict quality control was discontinued.

Each section had a "leader", experienced workers who inspected the job of the employees under them, while the whole staff was supposed to jointly train all newly hired people. After 40 days the

*"Soapbar" P 90 pickups.*

*1960 Gibson GA 40T amp.*

new woman or man was supposed to either have acquired the necessary skills for the job or quit. This combination of experienced individuals in key positions, motivated employees, skilled woodworkers, and musicians taking care of the quality control in a friendly but efficient organization, is what allowed Gibson, in the fifties, to become the undisputed leader in the field of musical instruments. They were aware of, but not afraid of competition, even when the new star, Leo Fender challenged all the established brands with his revolutionary concepts. Ted McCarty, however, admitted that Fender was the leader in the amplifier field, even if he did not personally like their "harsh sound".

Under McCarty's leadership, Gibson introduced the ES 175 (conceived of before his arrival), the first thinline models (including the ES 125T and the ES 350T), the Byrdland, the semi-solid ES 300 series, the solid body and other innovations.

*The Gibson factory in 1984. The Gibson brand was bought by Norlin Industries in 1969. In 1974 Norlin opened a new plant in Nashville, Tennessee, and in 1984 decided to close the doors of the historic factory in Kalamazoo. Jim Deurloo, Marv Lamb and J. P. Moat, with several employees, decided to stay and rented part of the plant founding Heritage in 1985, to continue the tradition of making great guitars in Kalamazoo.*

# Theodore Milson McCarty

Theodore "Ted" Milson McCarty was born on October 10, 1909, in Somerset, Kentucky. His mother died when he was only three years old, so his brother was raised by their grandmother, and Ted by her sister.

Frederick "Pop" Wrampelmeier and his wife Nora did not have children, so, even though they were far from rich, they did their best to be like real parents for Ted. They lived in Cincinnati and as a teen Ted got interested in crystal radio technology and built his first radio set. He studied in the industrial section of Withrow High School in Cincinnati and then attended engineering courses at the University of the same town, where he also excelled in sports and worked as a clerk, and then as manager of the bookstore.

He married Elinor Henrietta Bauer on June 14, 1935, but grew tired of his job and began to look for other opportunities.

In 1936 Ted joined the accounting department at the Rudolph Wurlitzer Company. Later he became Wurlitzer's Corporate Purchasing Agent, but after the war things became very hard in the music industry and McCarty was not satisfied with his position at Wurlitzer. The Company had a new Vice President and Ted did not get along well with him, so he resigned in 1947 looking for something outside of the music industry.

McCarty found an opportunity as assistant treasurer for the Brach Candy Company, but his friend Bill Gretsch insisted he must stay in the music industry and arranged a meeting with Maurice Berlin, the president of Chicago Musical Instruments, the company which owned the Gibson brand.

Maurice H. Berlin was born in Russia, and when his parents, who were very poor, arrived in the United States, he started working at the age of just twelve years old for Wurlitzer. With time he proved to be a very talented businessman and founded the Chicago Musical Instruments Company, which, during the war, acquired the Gibson brand. Smart but kind, he is recalled as a true gentleman and instead of being jealous of successful competitors like Leo Fender, he used to admire them.

In the late forties, Guy Hart, General Manager of Gibson since 1924, took over as President. He had health problems and his assistant at that time, Neil Abrams, died of a heart attack. The plant, which worked for the military industry during the war, needed reorganization. Maurice Berlin, who knew McCarty, heard that he was no longer with Wurlitzer, and didn't think twice about offering him to go to Kalamazoo as CEO to get the factory back on track.

*Ted McCarty holding the first all gold electric guitar, based on the ES 175, ordered by Les Paul for a disabled player, in 1951; the following year saw the introduction of the ES 295, essentially a gold finished, two pickups, ES 175. With McCarty are (left to right): Walter Fuller, Julius Bellson, Wilbur Marker and John Huis.*

McCarty started his new job in March 1948. His friendly attitude, enthusiasm, and ability motivated the workers and in May Gibson was again turning a profit. In 1950 Ted became the President of Gibson, the youngest in the industry. Berlin's understanding of the market and good relationship with McCarty were crucial in making Gibson so successful, many innovations and great models would never have been made if McCarty was not so wholeheartedly supported by Berlin.

*1952 Gibson ES 295.*

*1959 ES125T. The thin-line concept was one of McCarty's innovations.*

*1953 ES 175. Introduced in 1949 it quickly became a jazz player's workhorse.*

*1956 Les Paul Junior, 1956 Les Paul Special and 1959 Les Paul Junior.*

Thanks to the wisdom of those two men, Gibson introduced the Les Paul guitar, the Tune-O-Matic bridge, the ES 330, ES 335, ES 345 and ES 355, the Explorer, the Flying V, the Humbucking Pickup, and later the redesigned Les Paul Series with the SG body, as well as the Firebird Series, with its new mini-humbucking pickups. Gibson also purchased the Epiphone Company in 1957.

When introduced, the Flying V and the Explorer were not successful, but later became rock icons and influenced many builders, the Firebird gained its many fans thanks to its bright tone and sustain, but the real classics were the Tune-O-Matic Bridge, a true industry standard, and the ES 335TD.

McCarty designed the ES 335, as well as the pickguard mounted pickup for archtop guitars, which was nicknamed the McCarty Unit, and was available with one or two pickups. He also designed the Tune-O-Matic Bridge, the Explorer, the Flying V and the Moderne (which Gibson did not introduce until 1982). The ES 335TD, with two humbucking pickups, a simple but elegant shape, versatile tone and comfort (thanks to its light weight), is one of the most successful models ever introduced by Gibson. McCarty also designed the swing out arm of the Bigsby vibrato, which allowed the player to put it out of the way when not using it, for which he received a small royalty on any unit sold by Paul Bigsby.

In 1964 Arnie Berlin, the son of Maurice, became the new President at CMI, while his father remained as Chairman of the Board. McCarty did not like Arnie, nor the changes he brought to Gibson, saying that he had "no use for Arnie Berlin".

In 1965 McCarty resigned from Gibson and acquired the Bigsby Company; although he stayed in Kalamazoo until June 1966 to allow them time to find a replacement. In 1984 Gibson moved production to Nashville and three of the best woodworkers, Jim Deurloo, Marvin Lamb and J.P. Moats stayed behind, renting part of the old plant to found Heritage Guitars, and McCarty assisted them with the finances.

In 1966 McCarty became a consultant for Paul Reed Smith and in 1994; PRS Guitars launched a line of McCarty models.

However, we will let Ted McCarty himself tell us about his years at Gibson through one of his last interviews with our friend Pier Paolo Adda, a well-known musician and collector.

Pier Paolo met Ted McCarty at the Paul Reed Smith booth at the NAMM Show in Los Angeles, on Saturday, February 5th, 2000, and kindly allowed us to include the following exclusive interview.

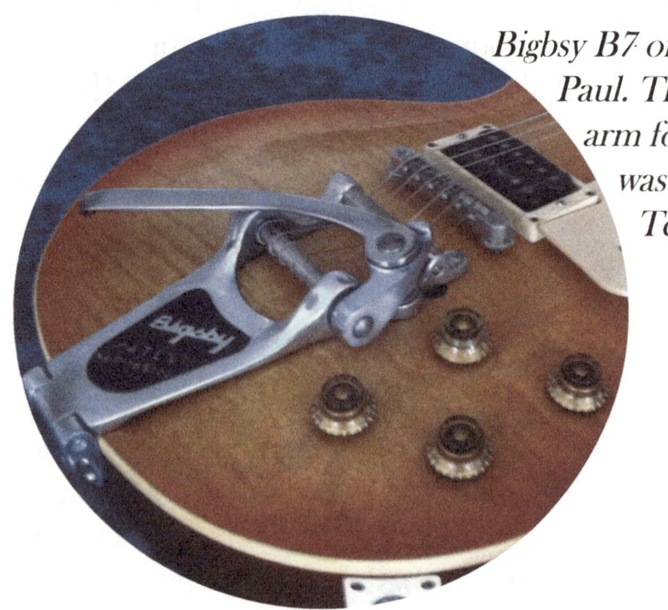


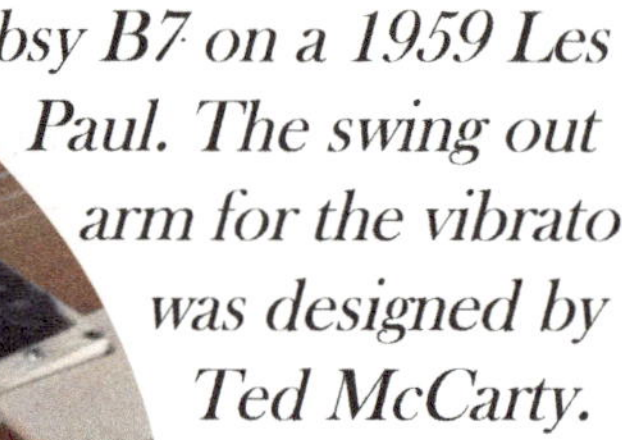

*Bigbsy B7 on a 1959 Les Paul. The swing out arm for the vibrato was designed by Ted McCarty.*

*Heritage H 535 (customized). McCarty assisted the new Company with the finances.*

*1960 Gibson ES 345TD. Introduced in 1959 with Stereo Varitone, these were meant to be used with Gibson stereo amps, as the 79RVT.*

# INTERVIEW

P. P. Adda - How do you do Mr. McCarty?

Ted McCarty - *Well, I'm in a wheelchair because I cannot walk anymore. Plus I'm almost blind.*

P. P. Adda - I'm Pier Paolo Adda from Italy and I would feel really honored to interview you, if you're not too tired

Ted McCarty - *I've been in several places, in Europe, but never in Italy. I was ready to go there to buy some guitars and other things, just after the war, but somebody was sent there and I lost my chance. I've been in this business for sixty and a half years. No, I'm not too tired, I'm ready.*

P. P. Adda - How did you start to work in the field of musical instruments?

Ted McCarty - *I graduated in engineering from Cincinnati University and became Sales Director of the University's bookstores, we had three of them with 24 employees, but I wanted to get out of that situation and Wurlitzer, do you know Wurlitzer?*

P. P. Adda - Of course I do.

Ted McCarty - *Well, Wurlitzer was hiring people for the company's stores. I applied for it as I had experience in retail sales. I got the job. I stayed with them for twelve years. During World War II I was sent with others to build robotized bombing systems for the Navy. We adapted an old piano factory to produce devices for bombers.*

*After the war I went back to Chicago, where I stayed for five years. I met Berlin there. Berlin and I were friends, as I had some business with him while I was working for Wurlitzer. He knew I left Wurlitzer because I wanted to do something else; I wanted to get out of the music industry.*

P. P. Adda - You wanted to get out? Incredible!

Ted McCarty - *Simply, in the days of the Great Depression, I didn't see a big future for that field. He said "you have years of experience that should not be wasted. I'd like you to go to Kalamazoo, in Michigan, on my account, and try to understand why I'm losing so much money". As you know he had acquired Gibson, during the war, and was trying to relaunch it. He said "Ted, go to Kalamazoo on my account and on my charge. Take all the time you need and try to understand why I'm losing money". He also said "There is a President there [Guy Hart], but you don't need to care*

*Some P.A.F. equipped Gibson guitar models, all from 1959.*

*ES 335TD*

*ES 175D*

*Les Paul Model*

*ES 350*

*about him. You will go as CEO (Chief Executive Officer) and you'll report to me on what you think". I went there, and after a week and a half I knew what the problem was: it was the President. Everybody hated him.*

P. P. Adda - You mean that people didn't work well because they were unhappy?

Ted McCarty - *Yes, exactly. I wrote everything down and gave my report to Berlin. Later he called me and said "Ted, if you feel you can do it, stay in the company as CEO and if you bring it to good standing in a reasonable time, you will become the new President".*
*I accepted and started working in March; it was around the middle of the month. In April we were still losing a bit, but in May we were again making some profit.*

P. P. Adda - You were able to change the situation in less than three months?

Ted McCarty - *Yes, and I stayed there for 18 and a half years. When I started it was a small factory, with a one-floor building in which 140 people were working. Mr. Berlin said "Ted, I want you to build a new office for you, increase the production, enlarge the plant, add whatever you need, air conditioning, etc." So we added another building, and, when I left the company, the factory had 300 employees and two buildings. Going back to when I started and the old President's method, he used to get in and walk between the employees, always complaining about something, they hated him. He was so disagreeable! So one day, it was September or October of the same year, we were in the same office, I got a call from Mr. Berlin who said "I want to find the President's resignation on my desk on Monday". I asked "When do you plan to come to tell him?" He replied "It's not necessary for me to come, you will tell him". So I did. He was my boss, can you imagine? So I started that new experience. As time went by I was happier with my relationship with Mr. Berlin. He was such a gentleman! I think he never spent more than one day per year in Kalamazoo. He used to say that there was no need for him to come by, as it was my job to take care of the plant! See, Gibson was a different company from CMI (Chicago Musical Instruments), Berlin's group, and Mr. Berlin was the main stockholder. Gibson was a company with great prestige, whose history dated back to 1894. I loved it, I was there for so many years, and when I left I went back to Chicago, where I had the opportunity to buy Paul Bigsby's Company. We're talking about 30 years ago.*

P. P. Adda - Yes, many years, but to me you still look brilliant.

Ted McCarty - *Thank you.*

P. P. Adda - When talking about the old guitars, everybody says, and I can't disagree, that they were very different than today's production, and that there's something magic in the old pickups, the wood, the way they were made. What do you really think about that?

Ted McCarty - *They were the best. You can feel it by the touch... the way the wood was cut... the finish... and the pickups were superb! The best in the world! There is one thing that Mr. Berlin told me "Ted, when I made you president, many people used to say "let see what it's going to end like". They expected the worst. Remember that your reputation depends on what you do... and I want the best". Do you see that solid body with the cutaway (points to a PRS McCarty)? Well, I introduced that kind of instrument in 1952.*

P. P. Adda - Sure, the Les Paul Model.

Ted McCarty - *That's why it's advertised as my model.*

P. P. Adda - But your name is in the guitar's history. It's significant.

Ted McCarty – *Yes.*

P. P. Adda - Mr. McCarty, who got the idea for the humbucking pickup?
Probably you had been asked that a thousand times, but please, be patient.

Ted McCarty - *I heard something. I was Gibson's President at the time. Some musicians said about our pickups "Ted, they're good, but sometimes, while we're playing, depending on where we play, there is interference, it comes through the amplifiers and makes a bad noise. We can't go on like that... it's a problem and should be fixed. And because of that noise, when it starts, it grows on itself. You must get rid of it". So I called one of our engineers, Seth Lover, we had very good engineers, and said to him "We must change this pickup; we must get rid of the noise". Well, he took the challenge and after 13 days came back to me and said "Ted, here is your humbucking pickup". And this is the name for that pickup since then, and its right even today. It works perfectly. It came out forty years ago from our laboratory and is still used. Everybody makes guitars in which they install humbucking pickups.*

P. P. Adda - But who got the idea for the two bobbins working against each other?

Ted McCarty - *In our factory we had a good laboratory and the engineers were very good. They took orders from me, the President, and they knew how to work. I gave the job to an engineer to solve the noise problem and he understood that in order to cancel the noise he had to put the bobbins one against the other. That's all.*

P. P. Adda - Very simple to say, but maybe much more difficult to actually find out how to solve the problem.

Ted McCarty - *Sure. We, for example, did lots of experiments working with Les Paul. One of them was about finding the right resonance, because if it was too much he would get mad. He didn't want it because when he was playing with the band and working on the strings didn't want the sustain to go on for the whole afternoon. So we took a piece of iron, from a train rail, put strings on that thing and did lots of experiments to find out how long they would resonate. We understood that the more dense the iron, the longer the strings would resonate. We could pluck the strings, go out for dinner and come back, and they were still sounding. We would take measurements about everything, try something, change, and try again, until we found what seemed to us to be the right resonance.*

P. P. Adda - A very compelling plan, really.

Ted McCarty - *Yes, just like Paul Reed Smith does with his products. He studies, tries, experiments and then goes on. He's not happy until he finds perfection. PRS is a great company. I'm very proud of how they work. Now seven of their models carry my name.*

P. P. Adda - Going back to your history with Gibson, when and why did you decide it was time to break the relationship?

Ted McCarty - *We had some different opinions about some of the choices made by CMI, then led by Arnie Berlin, the main stockholder of Gibson. One day Paul Bigsby, the producer of vibrato arms for guitars, whom I knew very well and whose products I used to buy for Gibson, called and told me "Ted, I want to retire, I want to sell, and my company is for sale". We were friends and used to talk clear, so I asked "Paul, what do you mean? You want me to buy it for Gibson or on a personal level?" Paul said "I hoped you would buy it, if Gibson did, I'm afraid no other company would use my products anymore". I asked if I was in competition with anybody else, but he said "I didn't talk to anybody yet, I want to sell it to you". I said "Listen, it's Tuesday now, I will be in your office by Saturday morning". He was in California, I was in Michigan. I talked about that phone call to my co-operator John Huis, a Dutchman, he was my right hand. He knew Paul very well and said "Did you talk to him on the phone? I would have been happy to say hello to him". I said "I'm going to California on Saturday, he wants to sell his company and I will go to talk with him, to see the situation. John said "I will go with you". So, we both went to California. Paul talked to us, said how much he wanted for his company. John was a good manufacturer, a factory man, not an office man. He checked how the factory was organized, what more was there compared to five years before, the last time he saw it. He said it was a good deal. We went out for lunch, John and I, and I said, "we'll buy it". I took 60%, John 40%, and when we came back to Kalamazoo we had no plant, no employees, but we were the owners of a company in California, whose buildings we had agreed to empty by the end of the year and it was already Thanksgiving Day! So we busied ourselves, found a convenient building, hired a couple of trucks, and had everything delivered there by January 1st. By January 11th we sent the first items.*

P. P. Adda - Do you remember what year it was?

Ted McCarty - *It was in 1965. So, we were in business, had the products, we carried on. When it was time to retire I asked my son and my daughter to sell the company but to keep the land and the buildings for me. Now I get a good rent and I'm satisfied. Everything concerning the vibrato arms I sold to Fred Gretsch, Fred Gretsch III. I've known the Gretsch family for 60 years. Me and Gretsch's actual President's father, Bill Gretsch, were good friends, and he was always telling me "Ted, when you make the decision to sell, let me know". When the time came I talked to him, he made me an offer and after some discussion, the company belonged to him. I think that now Gretsch guitars are built in Japan. Our Bigsby vibrato arms are used, I believe, on 14 different guitar models. Gretsch was our main customer and last October I invited Fred Gretsch to the party for my 90th birthday. He lives in Georgia, very far from Kalamazoo. I also invited Paul Smith. He came. Fred sent me one of the most beautiful Gretsch guitars I ever saw, with a gold Bigsby vibrato. He said, "that's my gift to you". But he didn't come to my party.*

P. P. Adda - Maybe he had some problems.

Ted McCarty - *Yes, there'd been some storms in his area, and the way was very long. It was a very good party, with just the right friends. We talked a lot. I went to Fred Gretsch's baptism, he's Catholic. His father and I were really good friends. So, when this President Fred Gretsch was baptized, they had a big party and I was invited. I was talking about that with Fred just this morning.*

P. P. Adda - I'd like to know how your collaboration with Paul Reed Smith started.

Ted McCarty - *The work with Paul? Well, one day I was sitting in my office, and Paul called and said "I'm Paul Reed Smith and I'm looking for someone who can help me with some problems", and he added "I've been looking through some patents on several objects related to guitars and your name came up often, and I found out that many things you patented are still in use".*

*Actually they were all useful things, still used, and really useful. In the end he asked me to work for him. He said "I'll pay you any amount you want, just let me know": I said "number one I can't come, my wife is sick and I can't go alone". He said "I'll come over". So we arranged an appointment and he came. He came to Kalamazoo with his factory's superintendent. So I told him how much I wanted for 8 hours and said to my employees that I would not take any calls or talk to anyone for 8 hours and would only talk with Paul.*

*He talked about his problems and I told him what I would do in that situation. My theory about industrial work is that, especially if you have to deal with thousands of employees, the first thing as you arrive you have to take off your overcoat and walk around the whole factory, talk to the employees, for example, if someone got a child ask how he's doing, talk to them all. To establish human relationships is very important, it's the best thing to do and that's what I did at Gibson to change it.*

P. P. Adda - When you arrived as CEO and then became President. And Paul? Was he happy with your meeting?

Ted McCarty - *Sure. See, just this morning, during breakfast, he told me "Ted, it took to me 15 years to convince myself that what you told me 15 years ago was right". One of his problems was that he couldn't produce enough pickups, I asked him how many girls he had to wind them, and he said "none". I asked "why?", he replied that he had men to make them. I said "how can you expect men to handle such fine wire? You need married women, used to sewing, used to delicate and patient work, who know how to use their fingers carefully".*

*A fine 1952 Les Paul Model in the brilliant, but rare, all gold finish.*

P. P. Adda - So this was the first advice you gave to Paul?

Ted McCarty - *Yes, he was making a mistake, only women can do that job with their fingers, not men. So this morning he told me "Ted, you were right". Now he got more women than ever in his factory and things improved, and the quality as well. I've been married. My wife is dead now, but with her I learned that women think in a different way. They're concerned about quality, do the job with care. And they learn better. Now Paul is happy, things are all right, we are good friends. We work together; if there are problems he can call me and get my opinion, for free. I don't charge Paul. A few months ago he called, he had problems with the chrome plating on the guitar bridges, I said he'd better change the chrome plater, so I told him about a very good gold plater in Michigan. I called that man, had some parts to chrome plate sent to him, then, after they reached an agreement about price, he sent them back to Paul. After two months I called Paul and asked him how the plating came out on the new bridges. He said "perfect". See, not everybody knows that some parts cannot be plated one time only; you need to plate them 3 times.*

*Now Paul introduced a new guitar and called it the Ted McCarty Model. He sent one to me, one to my son, one to my daughter and one to each of my nephews.*

P. P. Adda - A very good way to say "thank you".

Ted McCarty - *Oh yes, seven beautiful guitars and at home there is not even one guitar player. I said to my family, don't sell them, don't lose them, someday they will be worth a fortune. I'm sure.*

Ted McCarty passed away in April of 2001 at the age of 91, but his name remains forever tied to what is known as the golden age of Gibson electric guitars and many of the models introduced while he was President, from the ES 175 to the Firebird, are now highly sought after collector's items.

*Pier Paolo Adda and Ted McCarty.*

*1964 Gibson ES 335TD*

# Gibson And The Evolution Of Pickups For The Electric Guitar

*The ES 150, the first Gibson electric guitar.*

Since the twenties, many individuals were experimenting with ways to amplify a guitar by using electricity, and at Gibson, Lloyd Allayre Loar, a fine mandolin and guitar player, was a pioneer in the field. Loar was trying to build a piezoelectric pickup, but he had two problems. First, the technology of the time did not allow for the manufacturing of an efficient system, the pickup was too sensitive to humidity and the amplification rate was too low. Second, Gibson was not interested in what was still considered a mere novelty with no future as a commercial product. Loar left Gibson and later founded Vivi-Tone, producing the first electric piano, but it was too ahead of its time and the company faced financial failure.

In 1931 George Beauchamp and Paul Barth, with the help of Adolph Rickenbacker, built a pickup which can conceptually be considered the first modern magnetic pickup. It was called the "Horseshoe" Pickup, because of the shape of the two big tungsten magnets surrounding the coil, and was the first successful commercially available electric guitar pickup. The three men founded the Ro-Pat-In Corporation (ElectRo-Patent-Instruments), later renamed to the Rickenbacker Electro Company, and finally the Rickenbacker Manufacturing Corporation.

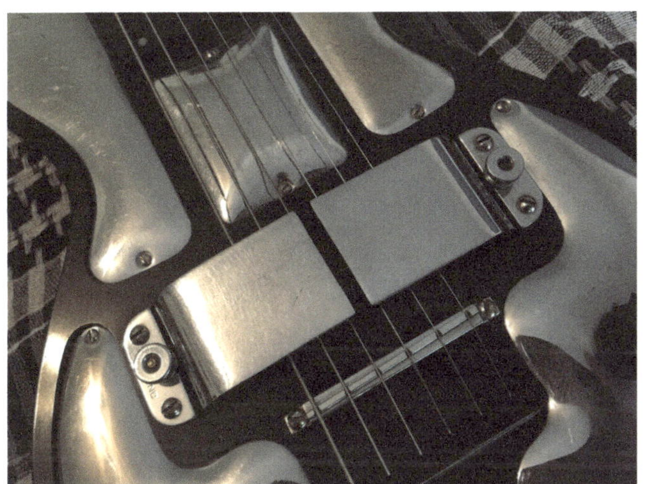

*Rickenbacker Horseshoe pickup on a B-6 Spanish guitar.*

The Horseshoe Pickup was used on a line of Rickenbacker lap steel guitars and was also sold as an aftermarket item to amplify archtops; at that point Gibson could not ignore the viability of an electric guitar any longer.

The first electric guitar "bar pickup" was introduced by Gibson in 1935 and made famous by Charlie Christian. Thus, it was nicknamed "The Charlie Christian Pickup". This pickup was first used on lap steels, then in the archtop ES 150, and was soon followed by the fancier ES 250. Loved even today by many jazz players, it was a rather bulky unit with long aluminum and cobalt magnets running parallel to the strings and placed under the top of the guitar.

They had a big coil of AWG 38 wire with a resistance of about 3.5kΩ and a nickel plated blade type pole-piece. In 1938 Gibson started experimenting with different gauges of wire, first using AWG 41 and then AWG 42 wire wound to about 9000 turns in 1939.

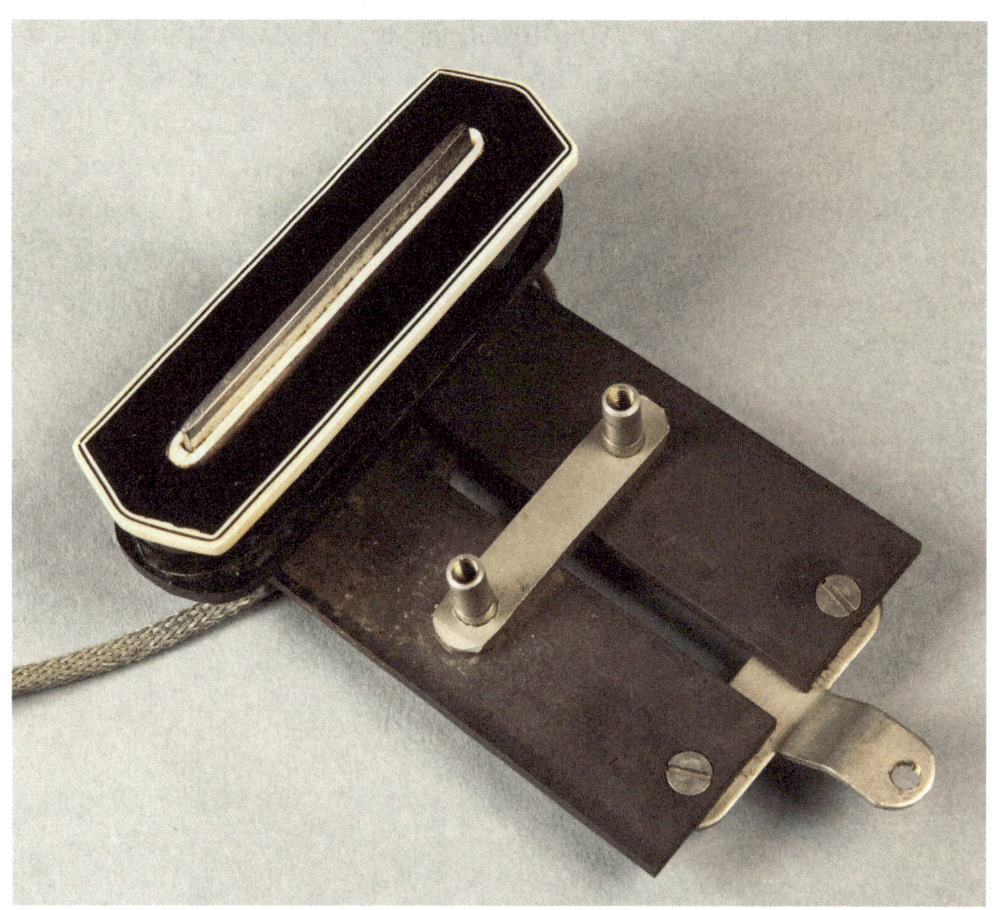

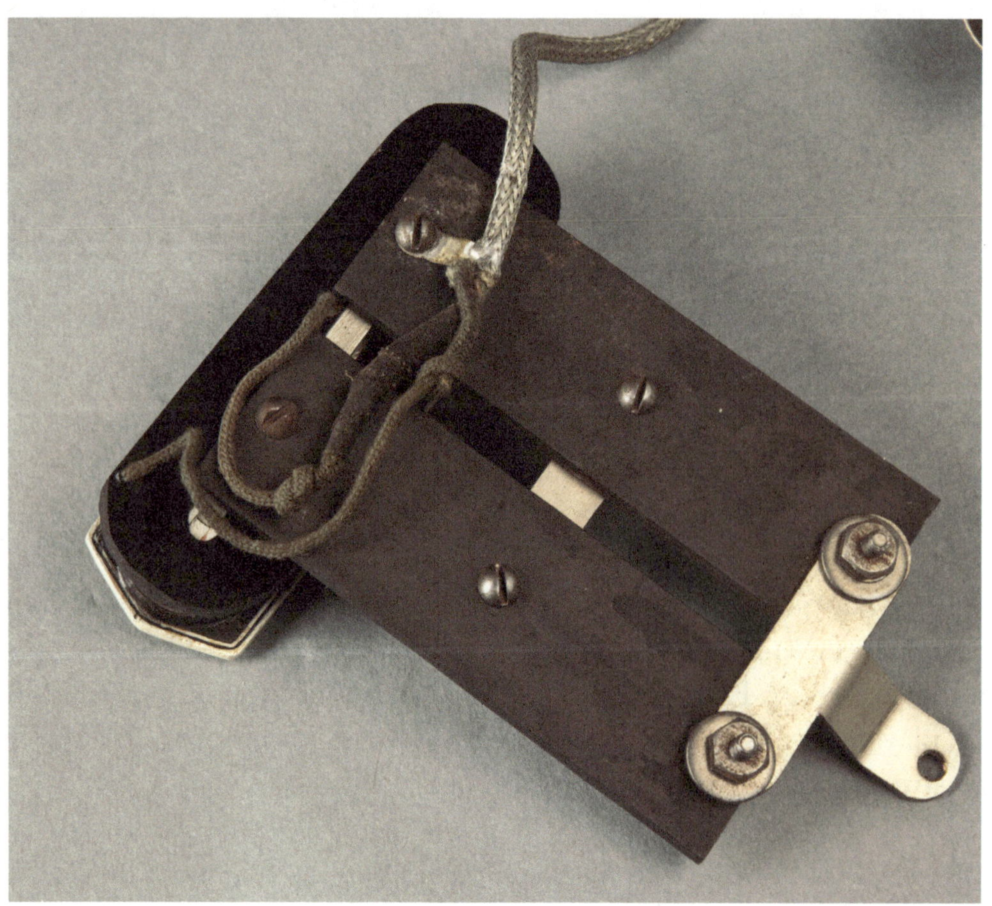

*The Gibson bar pickup, nicknamed "The Charlie Christian" pickup.*

While those pickups were made using permanent magnets, that, once charged, would keep their magnetism virtually forever, the Volu-Tone Company, in the late 30s, offered pickups to amplify guitars of any type, made with magnets that had to be charged before use. According to their literature, the use of permanent magnets was "old technology"! Those pickups had to be coupled with an amp made by Volu-Tone on which there was an extra input jack to charge the pickup which was supposed to last for about three hours. On the rear of the amplifier was an instruction sheet explaining how the system worked:

*"Plug AC power cable in to convenient receptacle. Insert instrument cable plug into energizing socket at extreme right. Remove guitar plug from energizing socket almost immediately. This energizes the strings, without which the Volu-Tone is inoperative. The energizing operation must be repeated every time a string is replaced. DANGER: do not permit the guitar plug to remain inserted in the energizing socket for longer than a second or two or harm to the instrument will result. Insert guitar plug into one of the sockets on the left. IT IS NOW READY FOR USE."*

A small label near the jack read:

*"Caution. Do not permit plug to remain inserted in this jack for longer than two seconds."*

The problem with the Volu-Tone pickups was that it was an inherently dangerous system, even though no injury to people or equipment is known to have been reported. Luckily the availability of safer and more efficient pickups made with permanent magnets soon made them obsolete.

In 1936, the Vega Company offered good quality archtop guitars fitted with a pickup called the Dual-tone, which was similar to the Rickenbacker unit but had two coils under the big horseshoe magnets, each with a bar magnet inside. The advertising explained: "The Vega dual-tone feature consists of two separate magnetic coils, designed to pick up string vibrations of varying tonal value". Rickenbacker used a similar configuration on their Combo 800 guitar of the fifties, which, when both coils were selected, achieved the humbucking effect. Interestingly Rickenbacker went back to a pure single coil design in 1957, just when Gretsch and Gibson were introducing guitars with humbucking pickups.

American wire gauge (AWG) is a measurement of wire diameter and in the beginning most pickups were made with a relatively thick wire, AWG 38 or AWG 41. During the forties, pickup designers started to use wire of a great variety of gauges to wind the coils depending on the output and tone they were looking for. So, for example, DeArmond used a wire as fine as AWG 44 on some models, while Paul Bigsby in 1947 was still making his famous pickups for his pedal steels and guitars using AWG 41 Plain Enamel (PE) wire.

Made with two AlNiCo magnets, one on each side of the coil, a "Charlie Christian" style blade pole piece, and wound for a resistance of about 3.5kΩ, the Bigsby model was not exactly the low-impedance unit Les Paul was always talking about. However, it was good enough to become his favorite lead pickup. It was installed in the bridge position of one of his Epiphone guitars and he used it on most of his hit records. It was also a favorite of Chet Atkins and Merle Travis. The pickup was shielded through a cast aluminum housing which made it the quietest model of the time, with a full, clear tone.

Later, Paul Bigsby kept the bigger wire but replaced the blade pole with individual pole pieces. On the earliest units the pole-pieces protruded through a flat cut in the cover, evidently having already been built for the blade type pole-piece. His lap steels continued to be fitted with the "Blade" model though. Fred Stuart, who makes replicas of the Bigsby pickup for Virtual Vintage Guitars, says:

*This pickup is quite a bit different than any other, in that the magnets are on either side of the coil, transmitting the lines of flux through a steel base plate and then up through the screw poles. This accounts for the different tonal quality and helps shield the coil at the same time. I wouldn't want to hazard a guess as to the magnet material, but the ones I've seen appear to be AlNiCo 5. As with anybody else at that time, supplies of that sort were a bit hit and miss, so I'm sure he would have used whatever was available. The toughest part of making these pickups is the covers. They are cast aluminum, and have to be hand worked to fit each dress ring. The shielding of the aluminum cover seems to filter out some of the highs, but the pickup has a very full-range tone, smooth across the spectrum, and it's quieter than most single coil pickups. I'm convinced that is because the impedance is lower (3.5 to 4.0k).*

Gibson initially seemed reluctant to get into the manufacturing of electric guitars, but after the success of the bar pickup had to keep its predominant position in the market.

The increasing competition forced the brand to keep experimenting; the main goal was to build a pickup with a distinctive and powerful tone while at the same time being smaller and lighter than

*Les Paul and Mary Ford, for them the best lead pickup was the Bigsby.*

*Gibson P 13 pickups.*

the bulky bar pickup. Gibson, in an effort to find a good balance between tone and power, experimented with different wire gauges and number of turns, and seemed to find the solution with 9000 turns of AWG 42 Plain Enamel wire, which became the standard wire used on Gibson pickups after 1939.

In the same year, a new magnet became available in which the main components were Aluminum, Nickel and Cobalt and hence they are referred to as AlNiCo magnets. These possessed a stronger magnetic flux than previous magnets thus allowing manufacturers to get the same power from smaller magnets.

The new pickups had a coil similar to the last version of the bar pickup, but used the new AlNiCo magnets and were covered by a metal casing for shielding purposes. Known as the P 13, it was, like the bar pickup, designed by Walter Fuller and produced in different versions for lap steels and guitars, with either a single "T" bar pole piece or adjustable screw-type pole pieces. Here is what Dave Stephens (Stephens Design Pickups) has to say about this model:

*The P 13s are some of the most fascinating of old Gibson pickups. They were made to replace the Charlie Christian pickup. The first one they did is called the "knuckle buster" it has a thick blade with big notches cut out of it for poles, the blade is cut short under the cover, so it has like a bit of a "T" shape. They used plain enamel 44 gauge wire on this one. They were so ridiculously insane to make, they only made a few. The bobbins were made of paper. Some magnets were varnished, and some I saw were wrapped in tape to stop microphonics. Then they went to a solid steel core in the center of the bobbin, and sunk pole screws into it, so you only see the pole screws; same paper bobbin but 42 gauge wire. Then they simply put a humbucker size magnet in the middle of the coil tilted up vertically as a blade pole. But with paper bobbins, lacquer potting, they were still too time-consuming to manufacture and the P 90 took over with a plastic bobbin, still a pole keeper bar on the bottom and pole screws. But there were also some early P 90s that had slug poles, and a few that had AlNiCo rods as well. They tried a lot of different things, for sure.*

The version with adjustable poles is the most well-known as it was standard equipment on the ES 125 guitar. Gibson then had to stop production during the war and by 1943 all electric guitar manufacturing was discontinued.

In fact, Gibson was not the first to use screw-type pole-pieces as Epiphone had launched a model in 1937 with that feature, called the "Master Pickup", and designed by Herb Sunshine.

In 1941 Gibson issued a big slanted pickup on the ES 300 guitar which extending from the fingerboard on the bass side, to the bridge on the treble side. It had a long coil, six magnets underneath (three on each side of the keeper bar), adjustable screw poles and a tortoise-like plastic top. It was designed to give a wider range of frequencies, similar to a smaller version of this model being used on lap steels.

*1941 Gibson ES 300 with the long Offset Adjustable pickup.*

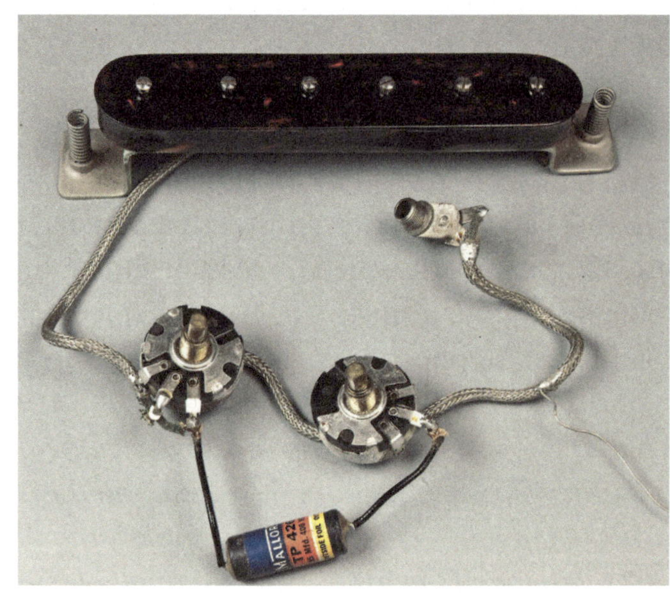

*The Offset Adjustable pickup.*

*A 1941 ES 300 with unusual blade pole Long Diagonal pickup.*

# 1941 LAP STEEL'S
## offset adjustable pick-up

*Top view of a 1941 Lap Steel Single Coil sitting on a narrow panel Fender Champ.*

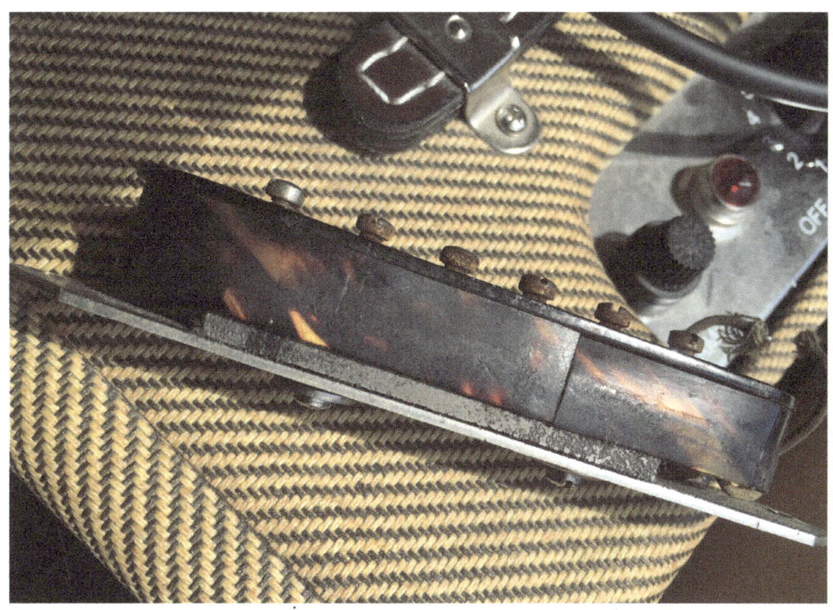

*Side view showing the bent celluloid glued case wrapped around the coil to protect it.*

*Showing the odd arrangement of 4 P 90 style bar magnets stacked in groups of two.*

*Showing the 4 bar magnets stacked in groups of two from an alternate angle.*

*Opposite page :*

*1941 Lap Steel Single Coil with casing opened with the internal coil visible.*
*The pickup has a thin steel keeper bar with turrets that rise up from it for every threaded pole screw section. Yellow celluloid plastic and glue remains deteriorated between the turrets.*
*It has an unpotted loosely wound coil, wrapped in masking tape and connected with non-waxed cloth covered stranded wire.*

The slanted pickup was not a success and was replaced after less than one year, by a new, smaller model which also had a tortoise-like plastic covering, but was installed near the bridge and slightly slanted (reminiscent of the Fender Telecaster which was invented nine years later). All the while, the metal covered P 13 was still in use on some guitars, and on lap steels.

After the war Gibson reorganized the plant and in 1946 introduced a new pickup, designed by Walter Fuller. Factory coded as the PU-90, the pickup had a plastic bobbin and a black plastic cover with distinctive "ears" on both ends to allow mounting on the top of the guitars (hence the nickname "Dog Ear"). The specs were about 10,000 turns of AWG 42 Plain Enamel wire with two AlNiCo bar magnets on the bottom. When the Les Paul Model was introduced, a version without "ears" was used. These had a square cover with rounded corners and was nicknamed the "Soap Bar". With the introduction of the P 90, the older metal covered P 13 pickups still in stock were sold to the Harmony Company.

The magnets used on the new model were thick AlNiCo 3 bar magnets, but during the '50s thinner AlNiCo 2 and 4 bar magnets became the standard. The new pickup was known as the P 90 and was used on many Gibson archtop guitars. It virtually became the "voice" of that brand for several years, representing that "smooth, warm tone" that McCarty was seeking, as opposed to what he referred to as the "trebly, harsh tone" of Fender pickups. These pickups quickly became a favorite of players from a wide range of styles; from jazz to country.

Clear, but strong in the bridge position and warm and full in the neck position of an archtop, the latter was also the inspiration for Leo Fender. Fender tried to emulate the tone of the P 90 on the neck pickup of his new solid body guitar (which was later known as the Telecaster) while seeking a brighter, lap steel-inspired tone for the bridge position. That configuration made the Broadcaster/Telecaster the first guitar with pickups specifically designed for the neck and bridge positions.

*1941 Gibson ES 300 with short off-set adjustable pick-up*

Leo Fender was making pickups for his lap steel guitars since 1946, but in 1950 added a metallic plate under the coil to enhance the magnetic field. This version became the bridge pickup for his solid body guitar named the Broadcaster, and then renamed to the Telecaster. A smaller unit, encased in a nickel cover, designed to mimic an archtop type sound, was used for the neck position. Fender pickups were structurally quite simple, compared to other brands, with six cylindrical AlNiCo magnets inserted directly into the coil, and top and bottom vulcanized fiber plates. For the Stratocaster pickups of 1954 this style was retained, albeit with the addition of a plastic cover and no metallic plate underneath.

In the new model Leo Fender tried to balance the output of each string using magnets of different height (i.e., staggered poles).

In 1955, increasing competition from Fender and DeArmond pushed Gibson to introduce something new. A popular DeArmond model, used by Gretsch and called the Dynasonic, had six adjustable cylindrical magnets in the coil, maintaining a clearer tone than the P 90 and a quicker attack due to the magnets' proximity to the strings, albeit not as powerful as the P 90 because a thinner wire was used. This model was known for having "the twang", as on Duane Eddy's records, who by the way used a Magnatone amp retrofitted with a 15" JBL speaker and a tweeter for a broader frequency response (most of the "twang" coming from that tweeter).

*Gibson "Dog ear" P 90 pick-up. (top)*

*View of the P 90's magnets. (bottom)*

*P 90 pick-ups on a 1956 Gibson ES 350.*

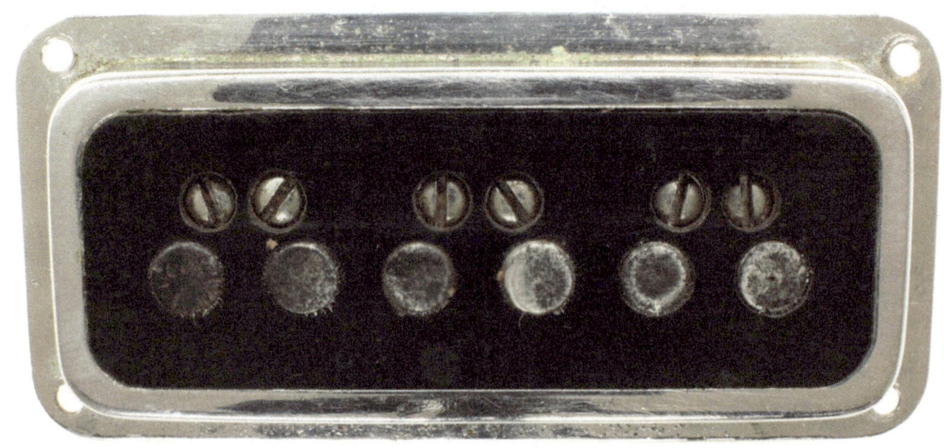

*DeArmond made Gretsch Dynasonic. A white top version of this pickup, called by the builder "Model 1000", was also used by Guild Guitars.*

*Gibson "AlNiCo" Pick-up on a 1956 Les Paul Custom.*

*Harmony H62 with Gibson P-13 pickups.*

*1956 Gibson Les Paul Custom with 1956 Fender Princeton Amp.*

To compete with the DeArmond pickup, Seth Lover designed a new unit, with six height adjustable rectangular AlNiCo 5 magnets and the same coil used for the P 90. With this design Lover achieved a sound with a stronger attack and more clarity, but still retaining the "voice" for which Gibson was famous. This pickup became known as the AlNiCo Model and was also known as "The Staple" pickup.

When Gibson introduced the Les Paul, the standard pickup was the single coil P 90.
Even if the bar pickup of the 30s had firmly established the electric guitar as a lead instrument, finally allowing it to share the spotlight with sax players, during the fifties the Gibson tone was that of the P 90. This tone was the sound of professionals. The AlNiCo pickup graced the most expensive archtops and was in the neck slot of the Les Paul Custom, but didn't last long enough to gain popularity, so, they finally decided that a new model was needed, one that retained that "voice" while eliminating noise owing to lightning systems and transformers. Seth Lover's task, essentially, was to make a pickup with the same sonic footprint of the P 90, but without the noise.

Seth Lover started working on the new 'hum-bucking' design in 1955, just a year after the introduction of the AlNiCo pickup, and it was first used on some lap steels in 1956. By 1957 these 'humbuckers' began to be used on most high-end guitars, replacing the AlNiCo model, while the less costly P 90 remained a stock item for lower-end guitar models.

*1961 Gibson Les Paul Special.*

*Gretsch Filter'Tron.*

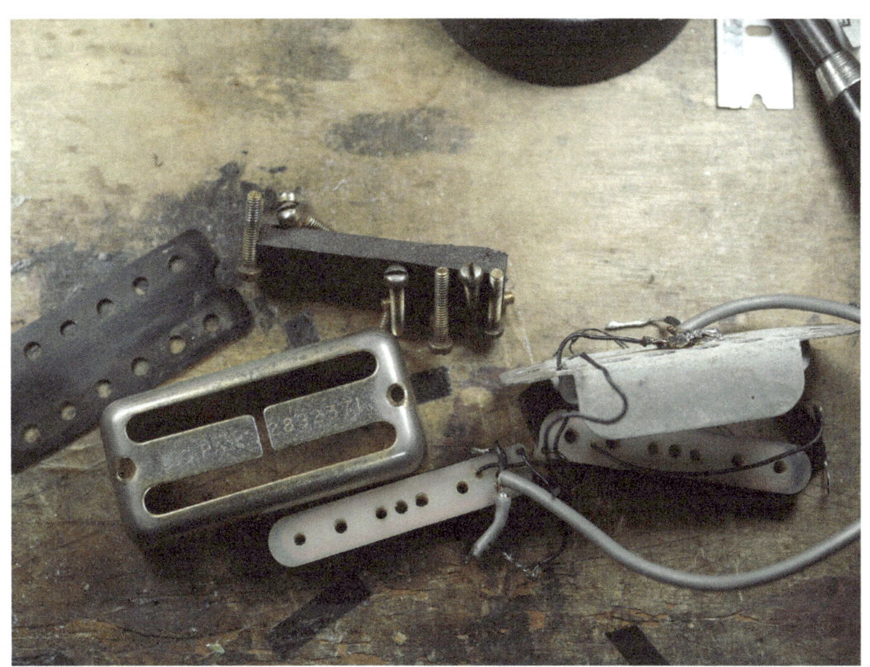

*Disassembled Gretsch Filter'Tron.*

*Gibson "P.A.F.".*

*Disassembled Gibson "P.A.F".*

# The Solid Body Guitar

*The "APP" Guitar.*

*O.W. Appleton.*

While Gibson was developing its "perfect" pickup, which was at the time represented by the P 90, the idea of a solid body guitar was becoming a reality. By the time Ted McCarty arrived at Gibson in 1948 at least two solid body guitars had already been created.

One, made by Orbra Wallace (O. W.) Appleton in 1941 or early 1942, had a pine body with a single cutaway and a shape quite similar to that of the future Les Paul (it essentially resembles a prototype for that model). The "APP" guitar even featured an arched top and the pickup, according to Appleton's son, was an older Gibson unit for which Appleton made a new cover, although the large bar pole piece suggests it was most likely an early Epiphone pickup.

Appleton claimed to have proposed his guitar to Gibson in 1943 only to get the answer that "nobody would play a solid body guitar". He claims that Gibson sent him a letter in 1952, when the Les Paul was first introduced in which they acknowledged the influence of "his guitar", but he just threw the letter in the trash.

In 1947 Paul Bigsby built a guitar for Merle Travis, and subsequently made several others for a group of select players (such as Grady Martin, Hank Garland, Joe Maphis, Butterball Paige, Billy Byrd, and a few others). Bigsby would only make instruments for players he respected and never attempted to manufacture them on a wide scale.

Bigsby's guitar had several features that we must call uncredited influences on later electric guitar designs. It had a maple body whose shape was not very dissimilar to that of the yet to come Les Paul. It also sported a headstock with six tuning machines on the bass side and a silhouette which looked like a fancier version of the one outlined by Leo Fender for the Stratocaster. Reportedly, Bigsby got very upset with Fender for not giving him credit for a design he thought was a copy of his headstock. Fender consistently denied this though, stating that their design was inspired by early European acoustic guitars such as the Stauffer.

Gibson and Fender, never cited Bigsby as an inspiration for their designs, but both were aware of his work. Merle Travis recalls that he loaned his Bigsby guitar to Leo Fender, who, on his own

*The 1946 Bigsby/Travis Guitar.*

Broadcaster, used the same three-way switch and Kluson machines that were used on the Bigsby guitar.

There are too many details to consider it as only being coincidental, but regardless, when in 1950 Leo Fender came out with his Broadcaster, McCarty and Berlin agreed that they had to have a solid body, too. The first prototype was realized in 1951, it was a very simple design, without a cutaway and without a maple cap, which they called the "Ranger".

A team led by Larry Allers was later put to work and McCarty announced that he wanted a guitar with a classic shape, a carved top, and a combination of woods, so that it would be different from anything else made and very difficult to copy by people lacking the proper machinery.

Ted McCarty used to call the Fender guitar the "canoe paddle" and he used to say that what made Gibson different was the arched top, while both the Bigsby and the Fender models had flat tops. So Gibson's solid body required an arched top to maintain that traditional element. Gibson had an automatic carving machine to rough-carve the tops of mandolins and archtop guitars, so it was simply natural that they would use it to carve the top of their new solid body guitar. The shape of the top-carve was then finalized by hand-sanding the top, so they were all slightly different from each other.

Mahogany and maple were the standard woods for Gibson, but what had yet to be determined was the proportion between the two for maximum tone and sustain, so there was a considerable amount of experimenting before deciding on the right combination.

In 1951 the first prototype was ready, but according to Ted McCarty several were made with tops of different thickness to find the right balance between the tone of the mahogany, the sustain from the maple and a reasonable overall weight, but those were just tried raw, and were never finished.

At that point they needed someone to promote the new instrument. Les Paul had tried to convince Gibson to make a solid body guitar before that was modeled on his "Log" guitar, but he did not have much success and so he continued to use guitars from his favorite brand: Epiphone. However, now McCarty had an opportunity to convince him to make the switch to Gibson. "The Log" was essentially a block of wood with archtop "wings" for more traditional aesthetics. It was a structure somewhat similar to that of the future ES 335 (a solid center block with archtop-like chambers), so, ironically, Lester William Polsfuss could have had more to do with the inspiration for that model than for the one carrying his own name.

Les Paul was recording in a hunting lodge in Pennsylvania when McCarty brought a prototype finished in sunburst, like their

*1953 Fender Telecaster.*

archtops. After Les and Mary had played a few runs on it, the agreement became simply a matter of writing down the details of the contract.

Les Paul would receive a 5% royalty on each instrument sold, and he also asked for a more rounded cutaway, a black finish for the standard version and a gold finish for a fancier version.
He also proposed a trapeze tailpiece which he had designed. McCarty agreed on almost everything, but decided that the normal version would get the gold finish and the fancier version, named the Les Paul Custom, the black finish with gold hardware, since black was considered the color of elegance.

Again, there is quite a bit of discrepancy as to who designed what, depending on who's telling the story. According to Les Paul, he was contacted directly by Maurice Berlin and got involved (and even loaned them some of his instruments) when they started to build the earliest prototypes.

From McCarty's accounting of the events, when he brought the finished prototype to Les, he was not aware of any earlier involvement in the project by the guitarist. In later interviews, McCarty said they made several prototypes with Les Paul, so it is likely that the guitar he brought with him was an early prototype and that they continued to experiment some more to refine the specs for the production model. That is most probably the point at which Les got involved. Whatever the story, one thing is certain, at Gibson they knew about Les Paul's interest in a solid body guitar and his experiments to that end. They were also aware of the guitars built by Appleton, Bigsby and Fender, so we can presume that any of those designs would have influenced the result somewhat, and the importance of Paul Bigsby as the most influential, individual builder of the time must not be overlooked. The Les Paul Model was introduced in 1952, with a mahogany neck and body, two-piece arched maple top, rosewood fingerboard, and a pair of P 90 pickups.

The Custom was introduced in 1954, with a mahogany neck, arched top mahogany body, ebony fingerboard, AlNiCo pickup in the neck position and a P 90 in the bridge position. The Custom was also equipped with the new Tune-O-Matic bridge, designed by Ted McCarty, which was later also used on the Les Paul Model. In 1957 the Les Paul Model received the new humbucking pickups and the Custom got three of them (with gold plated covers).
Two budget models were also added to complete the series: the Les Paul Junior in 1954 with a single P 90 pickup, and the Les Paul Special in 1955 with a pair of P 90 pickups. Both had a mahogany neck and body (without the carved top) and rosewood fingerboard. Double cut body styles for the Les Paul Junior and Les Paul Special were released in early 1958.
Also during 1958 a new finish was used on the Les Paul Model, a transparent cherry sunburst that revealed the sometimes rich figuring of the Michigan maple used for the tops.
McCarty said that he and John Huis had studied wood and often they, and a man appropriately named Stump, were able to tell from a distance if a tree would yield flamed wood just by looking at the bark.
This version of the Les Paul Model, renamed the Les Paul Standard in 1960, was destined to become a favorite among rock guitar players and was used on a multitude of classic recordings, establishing itself as the stuff of legends and becoming the most valued vintage electric guitar ever built.

*1952 Gibson Les Paul Model.*

*1954 Gibson Les Paul Custom.*

Even though many guitars were equipped with the humbucking pickup (for example, the ES 175, the L-5CES, the ES-5 Switchmaster, the ES 335, ES 345, ES 350, ES 355, and the Byrdland) and were played by a lot of jazz and blues musicians, when people talk about the Gibson humbucking pickup most of the time they are referring to the Les Paul.
Sadly some original ES 175 and ES 335 guitars have been robbed of their "Patent Applied For" humbuckers for use on some Les Paul replicas. Additionally, some of those pickups, if they had cream colored bobbins, were used to replace the black ones on some of the original Sunburst Les Pauls for a more fashionable look.

What's ironic is that the Les Paul came to fame after a failure, as the new sunburst finish was meant to revive declining sales and, since things did not improve, during 1960 the whole series was redesigned with a more sleek shape. After 1962, when the contract with Les Paul expired, it was renamed simply SG (Solid Guitar).

Gibson had referred to the lower range models in the Les Paul line since 1959 as SGs, with single or double (non-sculpted) cutaways, but now the reference was to the new, restyled line. Gibson started to put less emphasis on the association between Les Paul and the guitars because he was not as popular in the late fifties as when the model was first launched.

When it was time to renew the contract, Les Paul and Mary Ford had already decided to divorce, and the guitarist did not want to sign anything before things between them had been finalized. Ted McCarty claimed later that he made sure that Mary would continue to receive her share of the royalties. Les Paul, by the way, insisted in many interviews that he wanted his name out because he did not like the new shape of those restyled Les Paul guitars, but that was not true until several years later, at the time he did like them and wanted the new style guitars on the covers of his albums. Gibson was known for the carved top on the archtops and the Les Paul, so the new guitar had to have a different body than the simple flat "planks" the other builders had. Thus the sculpted horns and general outline of the SG were created (which was probably due to Larry Allers, who had been promoted to Chief Engineer at that time).

Les Paul's involvement in the design of the guitar carrying his name is controversial, as it seems he used to claim credit for almost everything, even if others recalled things differently. One thing is certain, and that is that he essentially designed and used special versions he had made for himself without the carved top and equipped with low impedance pickups that he designed and built with Wally Kamin. These were issued in the early seventies as the Les Paul Professional, Personal and Recording Models.

The pickups designed by Les Paul consisted of two coils stacked one on top of the other, each with a long AlNiCo 5 bar magnet inside, and separated by a plate. To achieve the low impedance he desired, about 300 turns of AWG 24 wire were used for each coil, with a total DC resistance barely reaching 5kΩ DCR with a 50Ω impedance.

*1957 Gibson Les Paul Custom.*

*1956 Gibson Les Paul Junior and 1959 Gibson Les Paul Junior.*

*1958 Gibson Les Paul Special.*

The units were then sealed in epoxy and enclosed in a black plastic cover. These were designed to be used by plugging them into the low impedance input of studio console boards. Those pickups would not work with conventional amplifiers, but Gibson designed a special 190-watt amplifier, the LP-12, with four 12" speakers and two high-frequency horns with low impedance inputs, for use with those guitars as well as with the matching low impedance Triumph bass. The higher-end Recording Model, however, came stock with a built in impedance converter to allow the use of conventional high impedance amps. A hi-low switch selected the desired impedance output.

Today Les Paul is known for the design of a guitar he probably didn't technically design, but deserves credit for several other important achievements. He asked Ampeg to develop the first multi-track recorders and built the most advanced recording studio of the time for Bing Crosby. He was a consultant for Jimi Hendrix during the recording of "Electric Ladyland". As a player he influenced countless guitarists including Jimmy Page and Jeff Beck and was a true pioneer in the use of effects. So the whole recording industry is in debt to him regardless of his actual contribution to the design of the Les Paul guitar.

*Gibson found the best tone balance combining a thick mahogany back and a thin, two piece arched maple top, as on this 1956 Les Paul Model.*

*1960 Gibson Les Paul Standard. The sunburst finish was introduced in 1958, revealing the two piece maple top.*

Only a few years later, players like Keith Richards, Jimmy Page, Michael Bloomfield, Peter Green and Eric Clapton recorded and performed with old style Les Pauls and the fate of the guitar was reversed. The guitar with a fading finish, fading sales and fading popularity, suddenly was resurrected and brought to the top. The "Patent Applied For" pickup became standard equipment on the ES 345 and ES 355 guitars favored by blues players. Jazz players appreciated the lack of noise they provided on models ranging from the ES 175, the comfortable ES 350, and L-5. However, installed on the Les Paul and matched to a roaring Marshall amp, P.A.F. pickups became the sound of rock and a legend in and of themselves, copied since by countless builders.

*A 1960 Les Paul standard nicknamed "The Giotto Les Paul" because it was found in Vicchio, birth town of the famous Italian painter. It is reputed to be one of the first Les Pauls officially imported in Italy.*

At the same time, during a tour in the UK, Sister Rosetta Tharpe showed up and popularized a Gibson SG shaped Les Paul Custom. Then Eric Clapton with Cream and Mick Taylor with the Rolling Stones used a wide variety of guitars from the old style Les Paul to the SG shaped Les Paul to the thin line models like the ES 335 and ES 355. In the Allman Brothers Band, Duane Allman was using a 1957 Gold Top P.A.F. equipped Les Paul while Dickey Betts was using a 1961 SG/Les Paul and by the early seventies, both models were extremely popular.

*1964 SG Custom.*

*1954 Gibson Les Paul Model.*

*1956 Gibson Les Paul Model.*

# The Humbucking Pickup

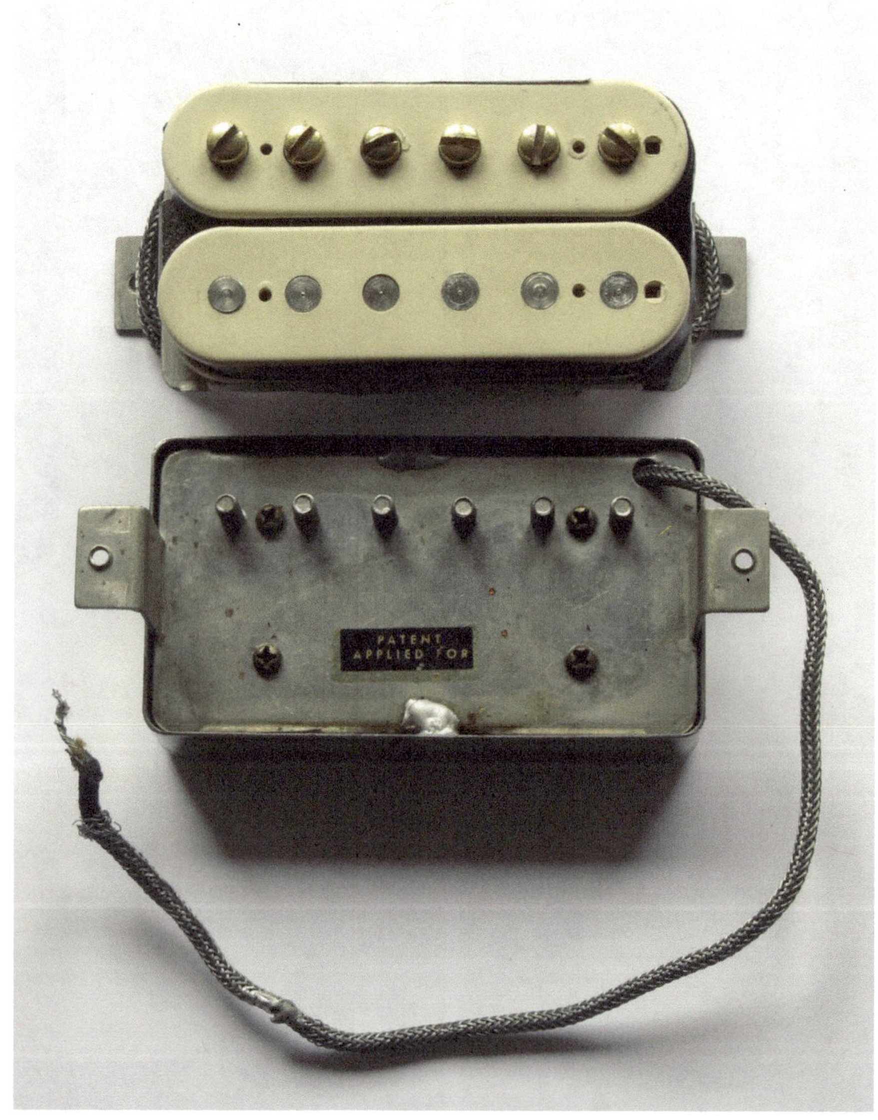


*1959 P.A.F.*

Single coil pickups can become noisy when near power transformers or other sources of interference and with the introduction of powerful amplifiers, like the Fender Twin Amp, hum became a problem.

Seth Edmund Lover had solved the problem in amplifiers designing a dual coil choke to reject hum, and tried a similar approach on pickups.

Lover started working on the project in late 1954, and in 1955 Gibson applied for a patent.
The principle behind the hum-canceling pickup was not entirely new, other patents had already been issued on hum-canceling designs. There was one in 1935 for Electro-Voice, another in 1938 for Armand F. Knoblaugh of Baldwin Pianos, and one in 1939 for Clarence W. Russell for a pickup with a horseshoe shaped permanent magnet. A pickup similar to Russell's horseshoe pickup with two coils was also used on Vega guitars in the late thirties. There was also a patent for Adolph Rickenbacker who had a pickup on his Combo 800 guitar with two coils; one for a darker sound and one for more brightness. When selected together, these coils acted much as a humbucker would.

What made Lover's solution different was not the principle per se, but the specific application for which the patent was granted. This application was the same reason for which Fred Gretsch got a similar patent on Ray Butts' design. This reasoning was that the noise from transformers or lights directly affects the pickup coils, but not the magnetic circuit; so, as two equal signals out-of-phase cancel each other with two coils connected out-of-phase, the noise is canceled. The signal of the strings, however, exciting the magnetic field, would not be canceled as the polarities of the magnet are opposed to the electrical phase, turning that signal from the strings back in phase. Connecting the coils in series would guarantee an output and tone fairly similar to the P 90, but without the hum.

While on the P 90 two magnets were used, in the humbucking model this newly improved design allowed them to use only one magnet, and it was put under the bobbins with the opposite polarities facing the pole-pieces fitted in each coil.
The coils were designed to have the same number of turns as a P 90, but split between the two bobbins, so instead of having 10,000 turns of AWG 42 Plain Enamel, the new pickup got 5,000 turns of the same wire on each bobbin.

Due to the distance between the two rows of poles, some of the string's vibrations get emphasized while some gets canceled, so, even if the sounds were somewhat similar, there would still be a difference in tone and dynamic range between the new pickup and the P 90. A metallic cover was further implemented to shield the unit and to protect the bobbins.

The prototype, now owned by Seymour Duncan, had six cylindrical non-adjustable poles in each bobbin and a nickel cover without holes, but it seemed a step back, since the P 90 had adjustable poles. So for the production unit it was decided to have adjustable poles on one of the bobbins, protruding through six holes in the new cover. Seth Lover called it the "humbucking" pickup and the factory code was PU-490.

At first Gibson did not use the new unit, the P 90 still being the main model and the AlNiCo pickup was standard equipment on the higher-end models like the L-5 CES and the Super 400 CES. In 1956 some lap steels received the humbucking pickup, but for some reason Gibson waited to install it on guitars.

*1959 Gibson ES175D*

# 1957 pre-decal P.A.F.

## pickup from an Electraharp Pedal Steel

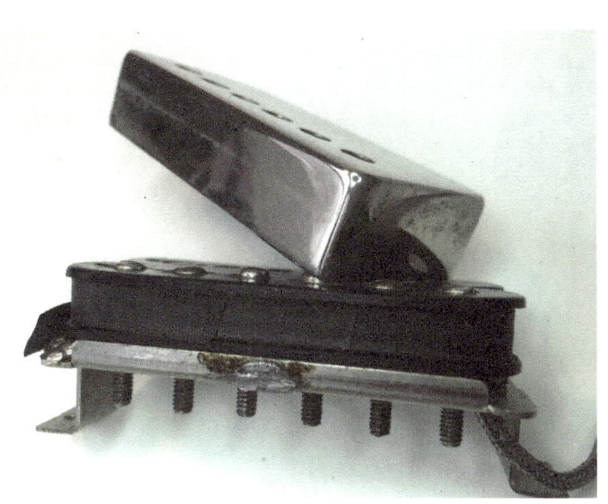

*With the cover just removed for the first time in 60 years.*

*Pre-decal 1957 P.A.F. from bottom showing the four steel bobbin screws as the solder is cut for examination.*

*Showing the dimples around the pole screw holes in the cover from a good light angle.*
*The cover from a different light angle appears to have no dimples in the photo.*

*Dark purple plain enamel wire shown through the bobbin windows of this 1957 P.A.F.. Note the very different style holes in the screw and slug bobbins.*
*Showing the dark purple wire in the bobbin windows from another angle of this 1957 P.A.F..*

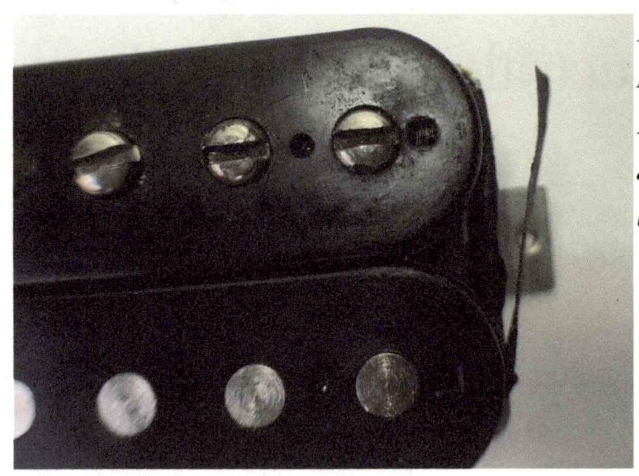

*Both bobbin windows of this 1957 P.A.F. have a square-in-a-circle shape to them but they are each very unique. Most fake P.A.F.s to date get these holes wrong and it is an easy way to spot one if they are not correct or are both the same.*

*Removing the outer tape protecting the hookup lead connections.*

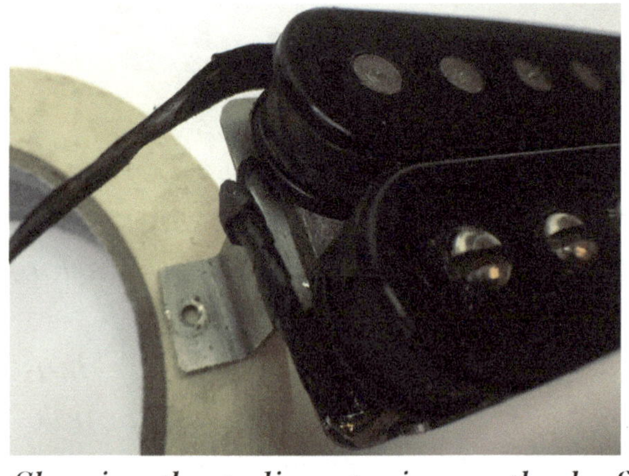

*Showing the tedious taping method of the inner conductor wire to the slug coil start and the careful taping of the coil finishes joint hidden behind the tape between the coils.*

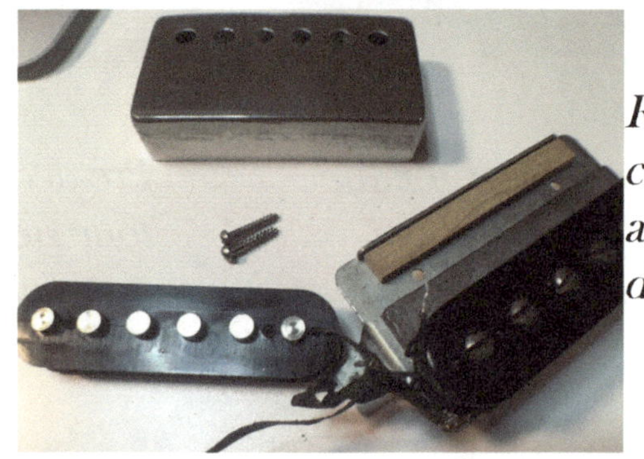

*Removing the slug coil shows the magnet and maple spacer underneath.*

*Showing the underside of the slug bobbin and two of the steel bobbin mounting screws.*
*Note that the parting pattern on each of the slugs is unique and rather crude.*

*Pre-decal 1957 P.A.F. magnet. Ground flat on only one surface, the other 5, including the side contacting the slugs, are very rough. This didn't matter on P-90s where the magnet contacted the pickup with only one face but matters on P.A.F.s where both polar surfaces make contact with other steel parts of the pickup.*

*Loosening the adhesive on the tape in preparation for removing it from this P.A.F. slug coil.*

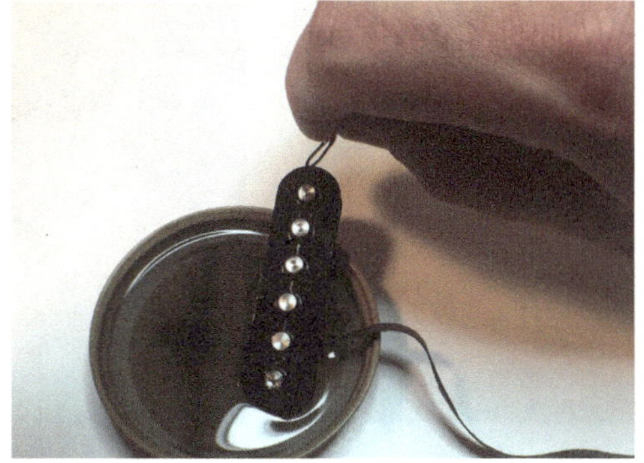

Slowly working the paper tape off the coil using a very mild solvent to not harm the wire or bobbin.

*Exposing the dark purple wire underneath the paper tape after 60 years of hiding.*

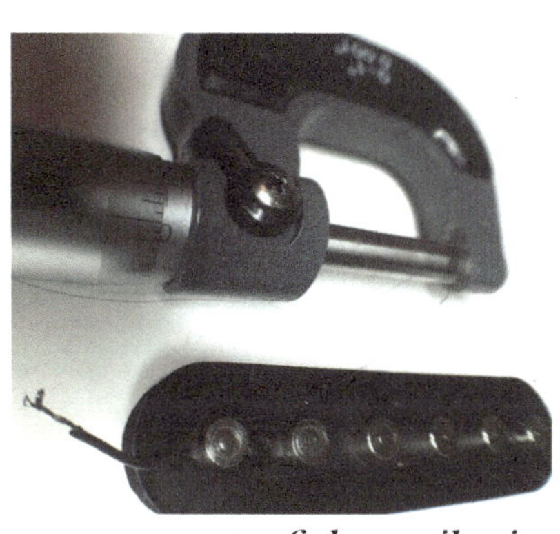

*Taking a sample micrometer measurement of the coil wire on this pre-decal 1957 P.A.F.*

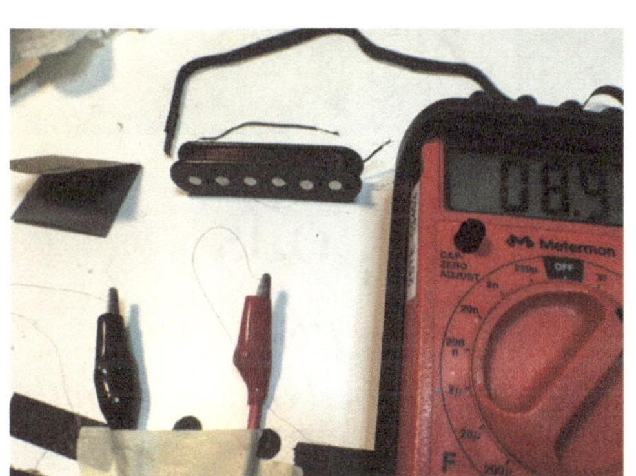


*Coil wire electrical analysis.*

*Measuring the thickness of the cover. Measuring at the edge gives a more true thickness of the original material, as the top surface is heavily hand processed.*

*Pre-decal 1957 P.A.F. in it's original state, before being removed from the pedal steel it originally shipped in.*

*Original controls of 1957 Gibson pedal steel.*

a

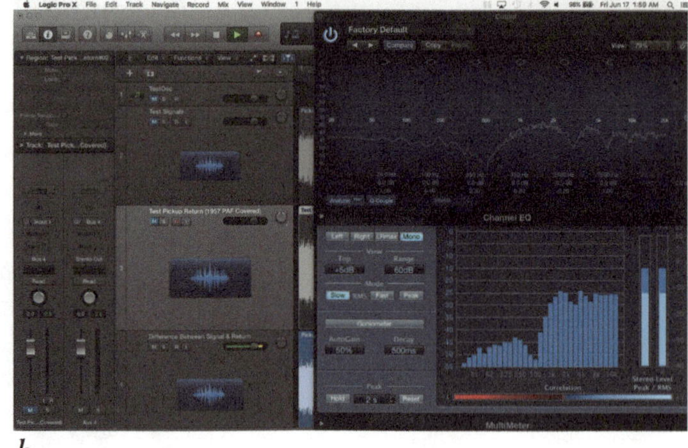


b

c

d

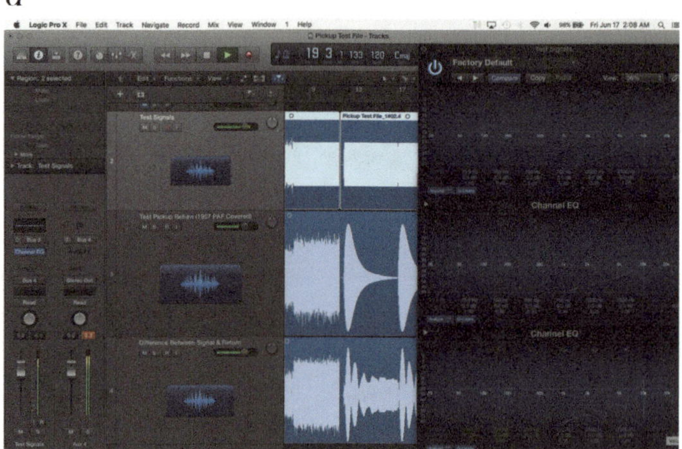


# Frequency Analysis of 1957 P.A.F. Coils

*a) The output frequency response of flat pink noise inducted into the coils of a 1957 P.A.F.*

*b) This graph shows the differences between the input test signal and the returned output from the 1957 P.A.F.*

*c) This screen shot of 1957 P.A.F. lower and mid frequency analysis from top to bottom: sine sweeps test signal, returned output from 1957 P.A.F., shows the difference between input and output signals.*

*d) This screen shot of 1957 P.A.F. mid and upper frequency analysis from top to bottom: sine sweeps test signal, returned output from 1957 P.A.F., shows the difference between input and output signals.*

The video is available at youtube.com/watch?v=LS6YgFALKjw&t=40s

At the same time, Chet Atkins (a consultant for Gretsch at the time), was not happy with the DeArmond Dynasonic and found a pickup maker, Ray Butts, who had just designed a model with a structure very similar to the Gibson humbucking pickup. The Butts pickup also had two coils with an AlNiCo magnet underneath. The main differences were fewer turns of AWG 42 wire in the coils, a slightly bigger bar magnet and six rows of adjustable poles in each bobbin, for an average DCR of about 4kΩ.

The sound of the Butts pickup was very clean and clear and in 1957 Atkins convinced Gretsch to introduce it on all the high-end guitars, replacing the Dyna-Sonic. This pickup became known as the Filter'Tron.

There is some controversy as to who really designed the humbucking pickup first. By issued patent number it seems that Ray Butts applied before Seth Lover, as Gretsch's patent was number 2,892,371 while Lover's was 2,896,491, but this is not proof that his design was invented first. Regardless, there is no evidence suggesting that the two inventors were aware that they were working on a similar project at the same time.

That same year, 1957, Gibson introduced Lover's humbucking pickup on its higher-end guitars, replacing the AlNiCo Model and demoting the P 90 for use on their lower-end models. The ES 175 was the first electric guitar to be equipped with Seth Lover's humbucking pickup.

The very first units came without any label on the bottom, but soon Gibson started to put a label with the words "Patent Applied For", hence the nickname of "P. A. F." given by collectors when referring to this pickup. The patent was granted on June 22, 1959 but Gibson continued to use the "Patent Applied For" stickers for a while.

*On original P.A.F.s, the label could be placed in different positions.*

# The Bobbins

The bobbins were black and made from Butyrate (Cellulose Acetate Butyrate or CAB, for short). In early 1959, the supplier ran short of black bobbins and delivered them in white color (they were in point of fact a sort of milky cream which eventually yellowed with age). This color change was not a problem for Gibson as covers were supposed to be kept on the pickups.

Those with the screw coil black and the slug coil cream are referred to as "zebras" and when the screw coil is cream they are called "reverse zebras"; for some unknown reason the "zebra" pickups are the more common of the two.

The relative rarity of double cream (also called "full cream") or zebra pickups with their visual appeal makes these more sought after and valued than the otherwise identical pickups with black bobbins.

So in 1959, starting around serial number 9 0600, the pickups could be double black, double white or zebra, with double whites more common after about serial number 9 1000 and double blacks again gaining dominance about serial number 9 1900. White bobbins did not disappear until late 1960. Unfortunately several Bursts have had original double black P.A.F.s replaced with the more fashionable double whites, which were probably taken out of other models, like the ES 175 or ES 335. The only way to make sure that a set of double whites is indigenous to a Burst is to inspect the soldering on the pots very carefully.

*P.A.F. bobbins were made from Cellulose Acetate Butyrate aka C.A.B.*

*Black P.A.F.*

*Cream P.A.F.*

*Zebra P.A.F.*

*Reverse Zebra P.A.F.*

*Covered P.A.F.*

# The Windings

Seth Lover, while experimenting for the new humbucking pickup, wound coils with 4200 turns as well as 6500 turns The prototype, now owned by Seymour Duncan, has been reported as measuring 7.3kΩ. When he finally had to define the specs, he specified 5000 turns of AWG 42 plain enamel for each bobbin.

Winding to a specific number of turns was not easy on a production line and Lover always said that the ladies in the electronics department simply wound the coils until the bobbins were as full as possible. Contrary to popular belief, the machines on which the bobbins were wound had counters, but is possible that they could not be stopped exactly at the targeted number due to mechanical limitations. The Geo-Stevens and Leesona winding machines used were built for general purposes and were used mainly to wind coils for large transformers and not for such specific applications as winding pickup bobbins. These machines had to be adapted for winding pickups, on which a very fine wire is used, so their precision was somewhat sacrificed.

However, let's take a closer look in detail at the different properties of P.A.F. coils and how they were made, as expertly explained by James Finnerty.

# The Wire Itself

Gibson used AWG 42 wire insulated with a single build (thin layer) of plain oleoresinous enamel (like varnish) for the coils of P.A.F.s. This wire was consistent for all P.A.F.s, but the variables within that stated specification of wire were not. There is more than enough room for electrical differences inside the tolerance of this wire to come through as sonic differences in a finished pickup containing thousands and thousands of turns of it.

The NEMA wire specification for AWG 42 wire starts at a bare copper core size of 0.0024" and a 1,504 ohms/1000ft. resistance. The NEMA specification for AWG 43 wire does not start until a bare copper core size of 0.0021" and a 1,922 ohms/1000ft. resistance. That difference in size and resistance adds up over the 10,000 or so turns of a P.A.F.'s coils to cause a significant difference in electrical readings and sonic qualities.

Though wire thickness, referring to the copper core and resistance per foot, is frequently talked about in P.A.F. discussions, often less talked about is the thickness of the enamel insulation outside the core. The enamel coating thickness alters how much space is between every wind of copper and the ones sitting next to it. Since increasing this insulation thickness creates more separation between the turns, it also increases the length of wire required to make one complete turn around all the previous turns inside it, making each new turn of wire increasingly longer than the last. This thickness creates a physically larger coil.

The NEMA specification for AWG 42 plain enamel single build overall diameter starts at 0.0026" and the specification for AWG 43 doesn't start until 0.0023" overall diameter. That difference, just as the differences in copper core thickness, adds up over the total of turns of wire used in a P.A.F. As insulation thickness is increased, the total length of wire used for the pickup is increased, each turn is physically separated more from the others and the coil is physically larger.

These variables in inductance, capacitance, resistance and coil size all translate to sonic differences, contributing, along with other variables, to the many voices of P.A.F.s. Today, this type of wire has much more precise tolerances and is sold in not only half gauges but those half gauges have also been further split in order to be more precise. It is also sold in what is referred to as "min-nom" and "nom-max" (meaning "minimum thickness through nominal thickness" and "nominal thickness through maximum thickness") for each half gauge of copper wire. This precision makes the wire spec today four times tighter than it was in the days of P.A.F. production.

The ReWind Electric vintage pickup reference data appears to show some trends in copper core and insulation thickness over different periods of Gibson's P.A.F. production, but there is still real overall consistency. The best method for truly refining the voice of an individual vintage coil being copied is to custom order the wire in large enough quantities where the wire manufacturer will build the wire to stated specifications and tolerances for both copper core thickness and overall insulation thickness.

*Maple spacer, magnet and keeper bar on a 1958 P.A.F.*

# Coil Winding Machines

According to Dave Stephens of "Stephens Design Pickups", all original P.A.F.s were machine wound on any Gibson pickups he analyzed. Even pickups as old as the "Charlie Christian" bar pickup, looked machine wound.

Gibson wound coils on P.A.F. bobbins with several different types of winding machines (e.g., Geo-Stevens, Leesona, and Meteor). These machines could have multiple independent winding stations, each of which used its own spool of wire to wind one coil at a time individually. Each station of each machine had individual controls for variables such as tension, wire feed position and turn count. Each machine also had controls for global variables across the entire machine. These controls could all be a little different, depending on the specific machine in question, but variables like turns per layer, the width of the wind pattern being laid down and the operating speed were uniformly available.

*Geo-Stevens model 115.*

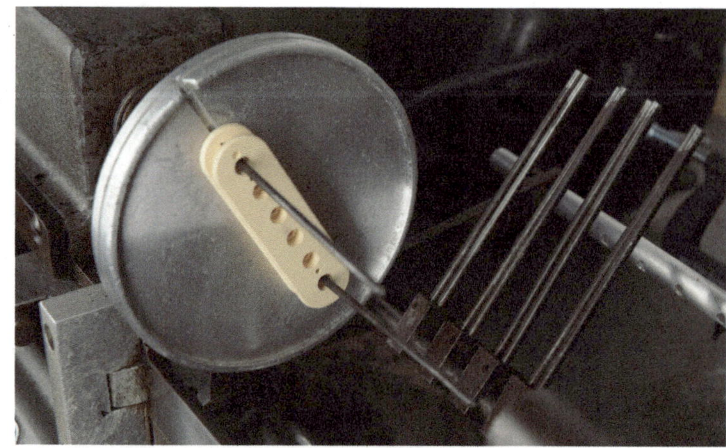

*Geo-Stevens model 115's wire guides.*

*The oldest winding machine in the Throbak collection used to make Gibson's single coil models and then converted to wind slug coils for P.A.F. pickups.*

*Leesona 102 B.*

*Setting the counter on the Leesona 102 B.*

*Jon Gundry working on the Meteor ME-301.*

The wire spools feeding the various winding stations of the various winding machines were regularly replaced as they were depleted. The setups and controls of the winding stations and entire winding machines were also adjusted and recalibrated regularly, as needed.

Jon Gundry of Throbak Electronics, who owns some of the original machines used in Kalamazoo, says:

*Gibson used four different machine models in the 1950s that I can confirm. I'm sure Gibson was very practical about these machines as tools to get the job of winding pickup coils done. However, differences between these machines in auto stop features or lack thereof and differences in fixtures, wire guides, traverse method and tensioning required for the different wire guides and fixtures put a tonal stamp on the pickups wound on these different machines.*

*Both of ThroBak's Leesona 102 winders produce tight coils with relatively little tension. Our Leesona 102 machines date from 1944 and 1957 and they are remarkably consistent in how they wind coils. The differences in machines have to do with models, cams and mounting fixtures. For example, when comparing the Leesona 102 to our KZ/LP-115 winder (Geo-Stevens Model 115), the KZ/LP-115 produces a much fatter coil than the Leesona 102 for the same number of turns. The KZ/LP-115 also requires more than twice the tension to make a coil compared to the Leesona 102. Tonally this translates to P.A.F.s wound on the KZ/LP-115 having a fatter tone than a pickup wound with the identical number of turns on the Leesona 102.*

Moreover, regarding how the machines affected later P.A.F.s and early "Patent Number" pickups adds:

*There are differences in how the internal start lead is handled and this affects the internal wire scatter as the bobbin is wound. However, these differences are a function of the machine used. In the later P.A.F. early Pat. # Era Gibson auto stop machines are more consistently in use, specifically the Leesona-102 and the Meteor 301 machines.*

*Gibson's choices when it came to P.A.F. pickup winding was a steady march towards increased efficiency. During the P.A.F. era Gibson used the KZ/LP-115 winder, the Leesona 102, the Slug 101 (a machine used to make P 90 bobbins and converted for use as a slug coils only winder during the P.A.F. era, likely used to wind older models like the long diagonal pickup and the "Charlie Christian") and the ME-301 machine.*

*All 4 of these machines produce distinctive and identifiable coils. Of these four machines the ME-301 is by far the most efficient and flexible. By the late 60s all pre-T-top pickups were wound on the ME-301. I have a photo from the late 60s showing 3 ME-301 machines in use at Gibson. It seems likely they purchased more of these machine sometime in the mid-60s.*

Of course other machines can be set up to wind bobbins with the proper geometry, as there is no magic in the machines themselves, but the historical importance of those tools cannot be denied.

Some winders who have been able to find other vintage models can testify as to how strongly they were built and how they can still be effectively used today.

## Starting The Coils

Naturally, every coil has a start and finish. The finish is usually pretty easy to find. It is where the coil winding machine stopped and the operator cut the very fine coil wire off from the spool that had fed that winding station. The end of that wire is soldered to a short length of larger stranded and insulated hookup wire. This hookup wire makes it possible to tape off and protect the fragile coil wire entirely and work with a more robust connection for assembling the pickup later.

Similarly, the start of each coil also has a connection just like this, but it is buried inside the coil. The way the start of the coil was hooked up on P.A.F.s is simply a perpetuation of how Gibson had done it previously on P 90s and pedal steel pickups. A more robust stranded and insulated length of wire, the same hookup wire used on the coil finishes, several inches long was inserted through the pickup, and left partially hanging out of a hole at the edge of the bobbin's lower flange, up into the coil-area of the bobbin.

The operator would connect this hookup wire to the finer plain enamel coil wire coming off of the spool and through the winding station's tensioner, traverse and feed. The operator would then rotate the bobbin and the thicker hookup wire first, then the normal coil wire, would get wrapped around the bobbin as the winding process started. The thicker hookup wire would get wrapped around the bobbin for nearly (and it varied) a full turn around the inside flange of the bobbin, and then buried under the rest of the coil. This turn or so of thicker hookup wire inside the coil changes the shape of the coil. Perhaps, more importantly, it uniquely changes the shape each time.

The exact way that the hookup wire, along with the solder joint to the coil start, and how the tape around it lays down on the bobbin, change the wire shape above them and will be slightly different from one pickup to the next. The wire may run on one side or the other, down the center or curve along one side or the other. The wire will also bulge up in areas and lay down in others as it is somewhat crushed by the tensioned coil wire wrapping a coil around it. Changing the shape of a coil inevitably alters its sonic properties.

Pairing up two unequally shaped coils in the same humbucker will create complex electrical and magnetic relationships, resulting in complex sonic relationships between the coils. In a guitar with four or six coils, in two or three humbuckers, the complexity is multiplied exponentially.

These random choices, again, add to the variety and uniqueness of the different P.A.F. voices produced.

*1960 Gibson P.A.F.*

# 1959 P.A.F.
## from a Gibson ES 345TD

*P.A.F. from 1959 ES-345 showing the iconic enamel decal.*

*Showing the thin tape protecting the hookup lead connections.*

*From the open side, showing the keeper bar, magnet and maple spacer.*

*Close up the decal.*

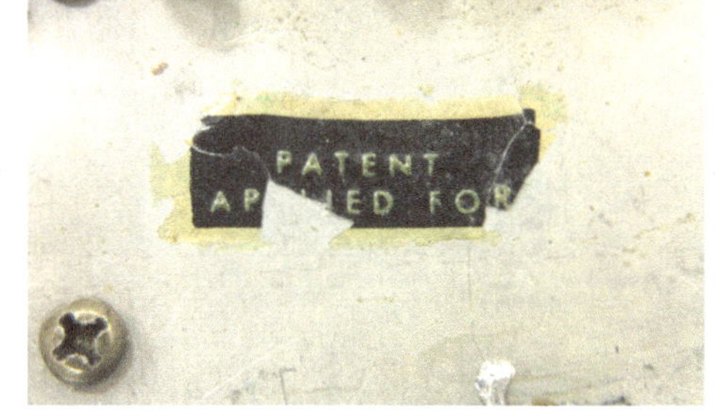

*Note the light circle shaped mark at the far left of the slug bobbin.*

*Showing the rusty color wire through the bobbin windows.*

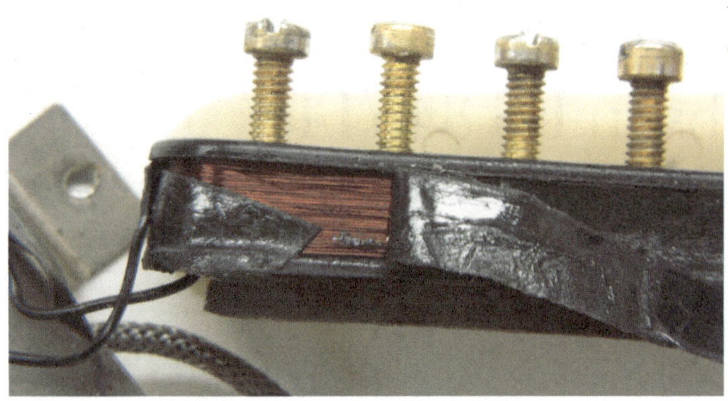

*Peeling back the tape exposes the rusty color plain enamel wire underneath.*

*With the tape removed, exposing the full coil.*

*Wire wrapping method around the slug coil finish hookup lead.*

*It is interesting to note that the top bobbin flange is beveled on the top side but not the coil side. The lower flange is the opposite.*

*With the pole screws raised up out of the bobbin, it is seen that they are gold plated and also unique in the shape of the screw heads.*

*The slightly green hue to the paper coil tape and the polished North side of the magnet exposed in this 1959 P.A.F.*

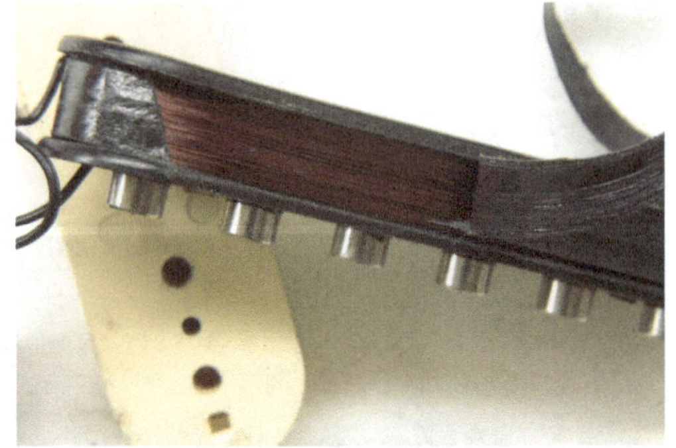

*The coil exposed showing the same rusty red wire.*

*In gold plated P.A.F.s, the slugs were still only nickel plated, as they were never intended to be seen.*

# Pairing Of The Coils

The data obtained during repair and investigation of vintage P.A.F. coils by ReWind Electric shows the various wire parameters, coil machine and setup patterns, and individual variance in the exact ways that the start wire was hooked up and laid inside the coils.

What is also shown is that the slug and screw coils of any given pickup are not always equal. They would have almost certainly been wound from different wire spools with different electrical specs, within the tolerance for gauge. The two coils of a humbucker are also likely to be wound on different winding stations, if not different machines entirely, and have their own tension, setup and alignment parameters, if not entirely different parameters inducing traverse throw distance and turns per layer, from having been wound on entirely different machines.

It seems that, during assembly, pickup coils were paired to each other the same way guitar pickups were paired with each other – with what appears to be little or no regard for sound or specification. Often the coils of a P.A.F. will share the same machine patterns and have similar coil shapes and wire parameters as each other. In other examples, however, the coils can be quite different from each other in the same pickup.

The Plain Enamel insulation gave the wire, generally, a dark brown color, that could change over the years, on some pickups appearing darker, and on some appearing more of a lighter shade of brown. The winding was done until the bobbin looked full and some think that there is a larger number of over-wound pickups with cream bobbins because the dark wire was more visible and made possible to make them full with more accuracy. However, measuring several double cream pickups, we found the same randomness as on those with black bobbins, so we think this is yet another myth surrounding the P.A.F.

Since the original pickups show a range between about 7kΩ to over 9kΩ, these values are often mistakenly used to guess the output of the pickup. In all actuality, in that the values are due to variances in the thickness of the wire or insulation used, the audible effect is much less noticeable than on modern pickups, on which the higher readings are due to more turns of modern wire with more consistent specs. As a matter of fact, some 7.2kΩ pickups could sound strong and full while an 8.7kΩ one might have a surprisingly clear tone.

The best way to get consistent readings would be to order the wire by ohms per foot, but that would be difficult to do so when producing thousands of pickups.

Here is an example to help clarify how DCR readings in a guitar pickup can be deceiving. These are actual measured results from coils wound at ReWind Electric, (i.e., we are not speculating for the sake of convenience).

Coil A:
Wire Used: Plain Enamel @ 1.7180 Ω/ft.
Turns: 6000
DCR: 4.36kΩ
Inductance: 1271.1 mH @ 120 Hz / 1504.6 mH @ 1kHz

Coil B:
Wire Used: Plain Enamel @ 1.5767 Ω/ft.
Turns: 6000
DCR: 4.16kΩ
Inductance: 1306.1 mH @ 120 Hz / 1310.1 mH @ 1kHz

Coils A and B have the same turn count, both are wound with what would be considered AWG 42 wire. The DCR is quite different, but the sound is nearly the same. A humbucker made of two A coils would have a DCR of 8.72kΩ. A humbucker made of two B coils would have a DCR of 8.32kΩ, but these two humbuckers would sound just about the same as each other.

Let's look at another pair made with the exact same wire spools:

Coil C:
Wire Used: Plain Enamel @ 1.5767 Ω/ft.
Turns: 5300
DCR: 3.49kΩ
Inductance: 996.7 mH @ 120 Hz / 970.6 mH @ 1kHz

Coil D:
Wire Used: Plain Enamel @ 1.7180 Ω/ft.
Turns: 4800
DCR: 3.49kΩ
Inductance: 827.3 mH @ 120 Hz / 826.7 mH @ 1kHz

In coils C and D it is obvious that the DCR is the same! However, look at the rest of the figures. The turn counts, and accordingly the sound, are VERY different! 500 turns per coil difference is significant.

Now take into consideration that these are individual coils of a humbucker. When two coils are

added in series (like a humbucker typically does) the DCR is doubled, and so are the DCR differences. In the example of coils C and D, if a humbucker is made with two C coils it would read 6.98kΩ total DCR and have a total of 10,600 turns. If a humbucker is made with two D coils it would also read 6.98kΩ total DCR but have a total of only 9,600 turns. Two pickups, both wound with AWG 42 wire with exactly identical DCR and 1000 turns of difference will sound VERY different but a meter or the manufacturer's specs will not offer a clue to that. Add to that that in Kalamazoo the coils were matched randomly. Moreover, we are not even discussing the inductance, capacitance and other parameters like turns per layer!
Add to this the fact that different magnets of different grades and charged to different specs could be used under each pair of coils, further emphasizing the differences in tone.

However, even if some got more turns of nominal size wire, a vintage humbucker would hardly be considered hot by modern standards. The coils must be the same in order to have the best humbucking effect, but even if this was not the case with the Gibson pickup, the hum rejection was still good enough that the human ear would not perceive any residual noise.

On Gibson pickups the wire was not hand-guided, but guided with a traverse which might need to be adjusted at various times while being fed to the bobbin with a uniform tension (the ladies would just check it by touching it with their fingers) but maintaining a characteristic irregular pattern due to inherent mechanical issues. The different shapes of the coils, made some think that they were hand wound, but while with hand-guiding the irregularities are more unpredictable, those induced by the machine follow a repeating pattern. This sort of "regular randomness" changes the distributed capacitance between the turns and decreases the inductance, raising the resonant peak.

In response to different machines and different adjustments, there are different patterns and so, different sounds, all else being equal (which we know now were not).
Usually the bobbins were wound separately and then randomly assembled, so it was possible to have noticeable differences in the resistance between them, that is why people talk about mismatched or offset coils in old P.A.F.s (the difference could be very small or several hundred ohms apart).

Some players prefer the tone of mismatched coils for a more open tone; with a character recalling that of a single coil, others prefer the smoother sound of more balanced bobbins (having them exactly the same was impossible at the time). Different samples from that era could have different turns per layer, different tension and different degrees of mismatch, so, even if they seem to share a somewhat common "voice", there is no single "P.A.F. tone", but a relatively broad range of similar tonal qualities.

# The Magnets

*Assorted bar magnets.*

The AlNiCo bar magnets used in P.A.F.s are the descendants of the P 90 magnets Gibson was already using at the time P.A.F.s went into production. These cast AlNiCo magnets were made by pouring molten metal alloys into molds made of greensand (silica sand bonded with Bentonite). The castings were subject to various heating and cooling stages processed to dimensional specification, as needed, and magnetized. Each P 90 has two cast AlNiCo bar magnets which are approximately 2 1/2" long by 1/2" wide by 1/8" tall. In the early 1950s, Gibson used 1/4" tall versions of these magnets in some P 90s.

*The M55 bar magnets used in P 90 and P.A.F. pickups measuring 2 1/2" x 1/2" x 1/8".*

P 90s have two cast bar magnets oriented with common poles (usually South) ground flat facing in towards each other and contacting the keeper bar (or pole shoe) under the coil. The outside poles of the magnets (usually North), contact nothing and for this reason the sand cast magnets are often left rough or unprocessed on this side as well as on the other four surfaces of the magnet not contacting the keeper bar. Only the point of contact was a critical surface for the design.

Each P.A.F., on the other hand, has only one of these bar magnets, or sometimes a slightly shorter version of it, only about 2 5/16" long, under both coils. On P.A.F.s, the magnets must fit precisely between, and contact, both the keeper bar at the base of the screw coil on one side (usually South) and the base of the six steel slugs in the slug coil on the other side (usually North). It is for this reason that Gibson eventually, though not initially, began to have both polar faces of the bar magnets ground flat with the North side marked, usually, with a pair of black lines. Some P.A.F.s, commonly in 1957 and as late as the early 1960s, used the earlier bar magnets made for P 90s which have only one polar face ground flat. During P.A.F. production (starting in late 1959) Gibson began using the shorter, around 2 5/16" long, bar magnets and those short magnets were seemingly used exclusively for a long time after P.A.F. production ended, as well.

The AlNiCo alloys varied throughout P 90 and P.A.F. production. There are several techniques that can be successfully employed for researching magnets, regarding their sonic contributions in pickups. ReWind Electric uses chemical makeup, graphing magnetic properties, and analysis of the physical structure, but perhaps the most important analysis tool used, however, is the reference recording library which contains, among other pickup audio test data, recordings of various magnets used in a static and known testing platform.

There is huge value in having the audio samples to compare to each other. They can also be used to later recall and compare the voice of a magnet that may have been destroyed or altered during the chemical makeup analysis or simply returned to its owner after pickup repair or evaluation work has been completed. So, there's a pool of data from the chemical makeup analysis, magnetic properties analysis and physical structure test results. There is also another pool of data from graphing results of the audio tests and listening notes taken during evaluations of the recordings. When combined, data from these pools shows patterns in the physical properties and resulting sonic voices of these magnets. Now, for ReWind Electric, this type of multi-layered analysis and comparison has become the core of creating custom AlNiCo blends and processes to reproduce these very special old magnets.

So, with all this magnet data, we can attempt to answer the very popular question, "What AlNiCo types did Gibson use for P.A.F.s?" There is a saying, "The only thing consistent about Gibson is inconsistency." Gibson used several types. The ReWind Electric data shows a great deal of A3s in the P 90s of the early 1950s and that trend continued into the early P.A.F.s in 1957 and 1958. A2 and A5 also show to be more prominently used towards the end of the 50s and into the 1960s.

The old magnets do not all sound the same for a given type. There are the thick and thin A3s, the thin A3s ground on only one polar face or both polar faces, as well as short and long A2s and A5s. Those size differences, especially when discussing the doubling of the magnetic material mass and polar face size in the case of the early A3s, will certainly account for sonic differences. Magnetic charge saturation, direction and uniformity create sonic differences, as well. What also accounts for sonic differences, and is often overlooked, are differences in materials and processes from one batch of cast AlNiCo to the next, even within the same AlNiCo type.

The data also shows that the composition and structure vary significantly with the old Gibson magnets. Varying the mixture of elements in the AlNiCo alloy will result in altered properties of the magnet. Additionally, there are some heating and cooling stages involved in the AlNiCo magnet manufacturing process and, if the timing and temperatures of these stages are varied, the resulting magnets can have altered properties. These types of minor changes can make several magnets, even all technically of the same type, sound different from one another when used in the same test rig. A2s can sound brighter or warmer, fatter or crisper. A3s can sound fuller or thinner, brighter or fatter. A5s can have more or less midrange or treble and varying output.

These variables are another reason why the multi-layered testing process and audio library are considered such valuable tools at ReWind. Using only a few sets of figures does not tell the whole story regarding these legendary magnets. Sometimes, in fact, it seems that the ears can see so much more than the laboratory machines and databases. The listening notes are often the best piece of data when trying to recreate the voice of a magnet. So, the question of what magnets Gibson used is answerable, but with a complex answer of, "several types, with physical and sonic variations within those types."

As we have seen, AlNiCo 3 was widely used on Gibson pickups up to the early fifties, Fender used the same grade in Telecaster bridge pickups (on neck pickups they would use A3 as well or A5) until switching to AlNiCo 5 in 1954 and on Stratocaster pickups until 1956.

We can only speculate as to why different builders at first used mainly A3, one of the reasons could be that A3 was less expensive. One of the elements in the formula for AlNiCo magnets is cobalt, present in different percentages in A2, A4 and A5, but missing in A3. Cobalt mainly comes from mines in Central African countries such as Congo and Zambia, so AlNiCo 5, which has the highest percentage of cobalt, was the most expensive.

Dave Stephens adds "AlNiCo 3 was used during the Korean War (1950-1953) because cobalt was a "war mineral" and magnet makers had no access to it. So, A3 was called "ALNI" because there was no "CO" as in cobalt". When the P.A.F. was produced, the A3 was no longer the main magnet used at Gibson, even though it is possible that some leftover A3 bar magnets could have been put in a few pickups.

Gibson called the bar magnet used on P 90s and P.A.F. pickups the M 55, referring to the size and bearing no relation to the actual formula, so an M 55 bar could be made of any of the AlNiCo types used at the time. By late 1959 a new shorter bar began to be used in P.A.F. pickups in AlNiCo 2 or 5 (in 1959 a new pickup was designed for the Melody Maker guitar, a single coil with the magnet inside the bobbin and so used a bar slightly shorter than the M 55 bar. This magnet was identified as M 56 and soon, to standardize production, M 56 magnets have been used for all the pickup models).
AlNiCo magnets can come in two types, un-oriented, or oriented. Un-oriented magnets can be magnetized in any direction, oriented magnets can only be magnetized in one direction (but usually give a stronger magnetic field).

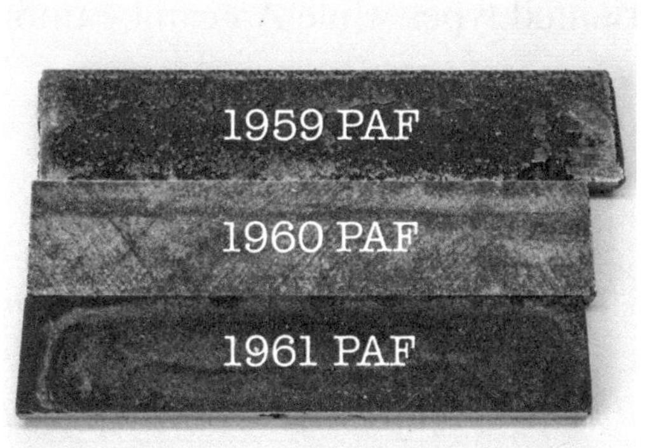


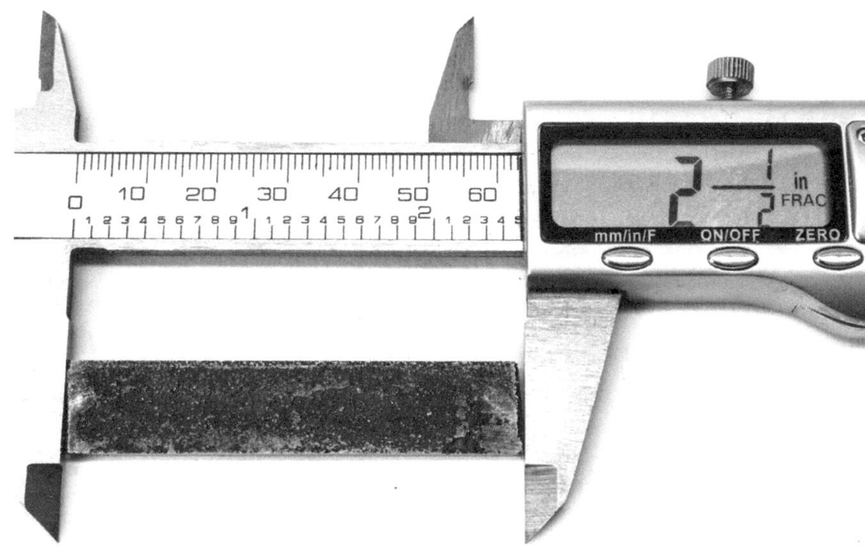


*P.A.F. magnets.*
*It should be noted that the year of the pickup, or order of production, does not necessarily dictate the size of the magnet, as a rule. It happens that in these photos the 1959 magnet is longest, the 1960 is a bit shorter, and the 1961 is even shorter still but it's also true that other P.A.F.s from those years are not always consistent in magnet length. On the other hand, it does seem true that towards the middle and late 1960's, magnets became consistently shorter than earlier ones, and it is also true that the earliest P-90s all used full-length 2 1/2" magnets.*

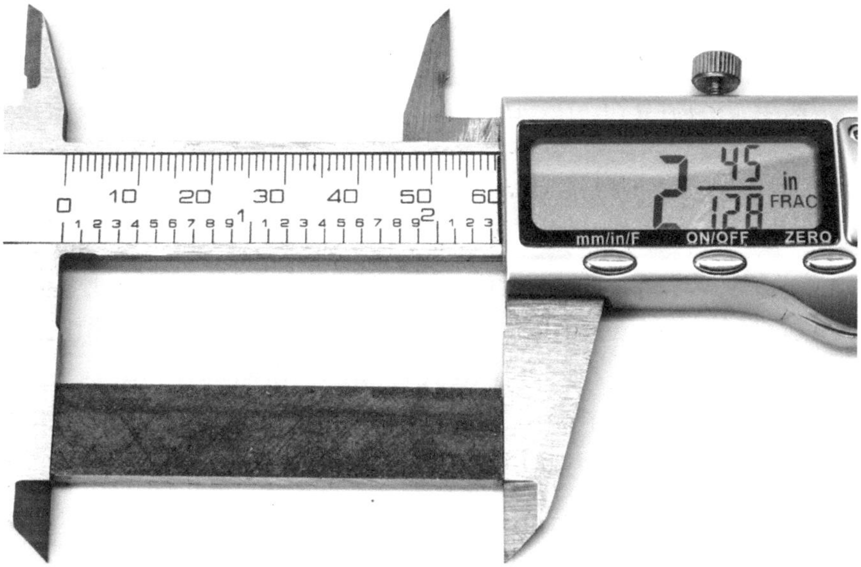

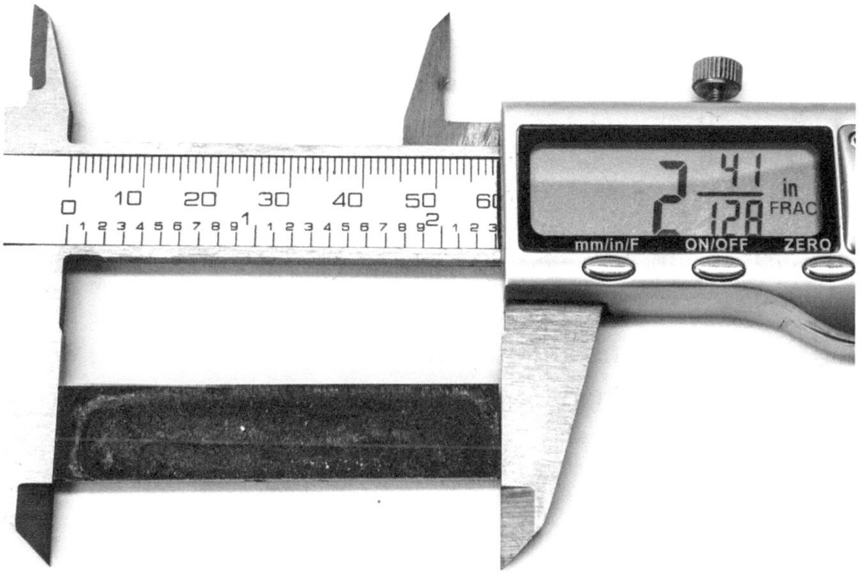

As used on guitar pickups, A2, A3, and A4 are all of the un-oriented types while A5 can be unoriented or oriented.

Bill Megela of Electric City Pickups says:

*I have found that, for instance, AlNiCo 4 was used more in certain years with Gibson. With regard to AlNiCo 3 I have not seen any pickups that have used it after 1960. I'm told that some do exist, but I have never verified one myself. Prior to 1960, when Gibson was using the longer magnets, un-oriented A5 was more prevalent than oriented A5, but after that, the short mag era, oriented A5 was used, and also short A2 magnets which I've found more of than A5.*

There is evidence that some old magnets have lost charge over time and Jon Gundry explains why that could happen:

*"Gibson charged magnets in-house with a rig made with car batteries designed by an employee named Glen Seybert who also made the traverse mechanism for the Slug-101 P.A.F. winder. Gibson charged magnets in small stacks and the effect of this is the magnets were not evenly or fully saturated with a charge through the stack. For best stability AlNiCo needs to be fully saturated with a charge. It is cheaper to order magnets uncharged which certainly made sense for Gibson, but their charging method left the magnets less stable and prone to losing charge".*

On the ES 345 TD and the ES 355 TD-SV the neck pickup had the magnet flipped for an out-of-phase sound when they were selected together and the guitar connected to a single amp's input through a mono cord. However, since most amplifiers have the channels out-of-phase, when connected through both channels of an amp such as a Fender Twin, or in stereo through two amps, the result is that they would be back in phase.

These guitars were initially designed for use with Gibson's stereo amps, like the GA 83, GA 79 and GA 88 and a special stereo cable had to be used. Many players had their ES 345 and ES 355 rewired for mono with the neck magnet flipped back in phase with the other. Another example of flipped magnets is in the Les Paul Custom, on which three pickups were used and when the selector was in the center position the middle unit was selected with the bridge unit (sometimes, on some guitars, with the neck unit) giving an out-of-phase tone.

Even after the introduction of the M 56 magnet, Gibson continued to use leftover M 55 magnets, so occasionally those could be found in later P.A.F.s as well as on some "Patent Number" pickups.

The most high-end guitars, with gold plated hardware, were produced in less quantity than the others, so it seems that gold plated pickups were stocked for a longer time, that is why leftover long magnet P.A.F. pickups with gold covers are sometimes found on guitars as late as 1965.

# 1959 P.A.F.

*1959 P.A.F., covered, front view.*

*...covered, front view, alternate angle.*

*...covered, front view, second alternate angle.*

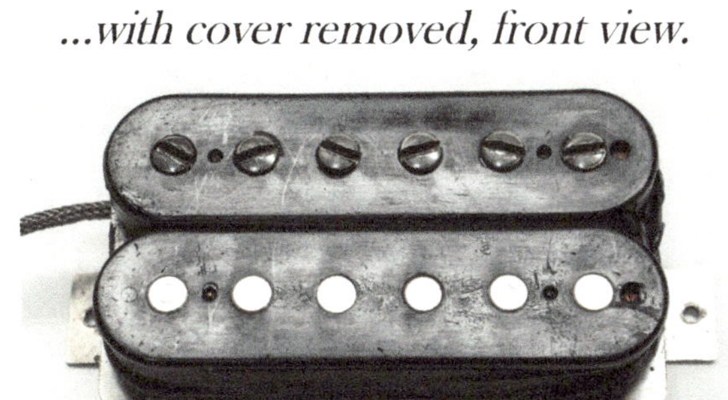

*...with cover removed, front view.*

*...with cover removed, front view, alternate angle.*

*...with cover removed, front view, second alternate angle.*

*...back view.*

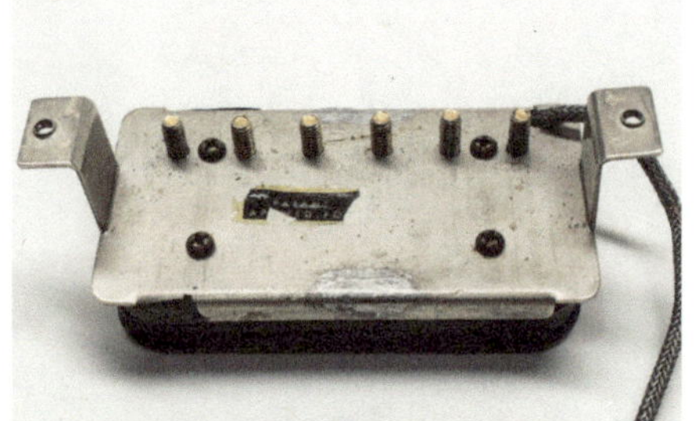

*...back view, alternate angle.*

*...cover, inside view showing the surface around the pole pieces is flat, proving the dimples are a result of grinding and polishing, rather than worn punch tooling.*

*...cover, front view, showing the strong dimples present around the pole screw holes.*

*...wire exit hole. Note the very particular spacing of the hole, and its relationship to the bent edge of the baseplate. The hole and the bend interact with each other, forming a uniquely shaped hole, where they intersect.*

*...cover, alternate views.*

*...foot, alternate view.*

*...foot, showing the deep "L" tooling marks.*

*...other foot, showing the "L" tooling marks.*

...decal.

...different views of foot showing the "L" tooling marks.

...bobbin windows, showing the rusty colored plain enamel wire through the uniquely shaped "square in a circle" holes in the butyrate bobbin..... alternate angle.

...showing the brass bobbin mounting screw, through the top hole of the slug bobbin. Note the tooling marks from the "corrected" hole placement.

...slug bobbin, showing pitting in the butyrate material.

...hookup lead connections. Note that only the thin tape was used on this example and that the coils start and finish leads protrude from the top of the tape. These leads more typically protrude from the lower side of the tape.

*...side view, showing the very rough surface of the magnet and the two coils being slightly different sizes. Interesting to note is that the physically larger screw coil has a lower DCR than the physically smaller slug coil, ruling out the possibility of a greater turn count on the screw coil accounting for the larger size. The physical size discrepancy is due to inconsistency in the thickness of the wire, not loose turn counts.*

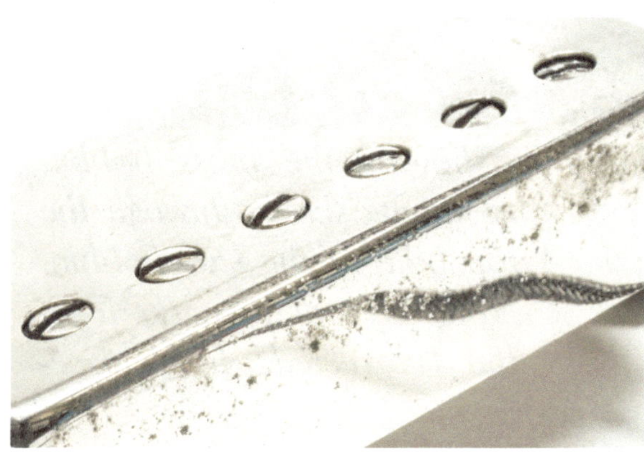

*...covered, front views of pole screw tops.*

*...covered, back view of pole screw tops.*

*...covered, side view of pole screw tops.*

*...covered alternate back view of pole screw tops.*

# Pole Pieces And Other Metallic Components

After winding, the bobbins and magnets were then assembled on a base made from German Silver, an alloy of steel, nickel and other metallic elements such as copper and carbon. A pierced support, called the keeper, was put under the bobbin, with the adjustable poles protruding through it and holes on the base plate, and one made from maple under the slug bobbin. The bobbins were secured to the base plate using four Phillips head screws, brass on earlier units, then nickel. Two legs on the sides of the base plates allowed installation of the pickup to plastic rings and for adjustment of the height of the unit using two long screws.

In this case too, the analyses have shown that the alloys for the materials used to make all the metallic parts, base, keeper, poles, were different than what is used today. Even at the time there were some differences in the formulas from one batch to the other.

These details are more important than the non-expert may think, as these components are, with the windings, part of the whole magnetic circuit and their characteristics have an audible effect on the tone. The actual alloy of metallic items changes over the years as industries develop and only recently, several winders have had the old components analyzed and conducted experiments to determine their effect on the sound.

Bill Megela from Electric City Pickups explains:

*With regard to humbuckers you have pole screws, slugs, and a pole shoe (keeper bar). I've had metal analysis done on these components and found that most are very low carbon steel, whereas most modern humbuckers are made with just low carbon steel. There's much more to this than just the carbon as there are other elements in the different grades of low carbon steel that affect tone, but for now we'll talk about carbon. In general the lower the carbon the more organic and rounder the tone, and the higher the level the more the treble becomes more piercing and the more sterile and harder the sound becomes. Granted this is just a general rule as there are many other factors that come into play here.*

Finally, the pickup is encased in a nickel silver cover, meant to protect the bobbins and shield the whole unit from noise sources such as neon lights. The cover is plated in nickel or gold to match the hardware on the guitar.

Even though the material for the covers was chosen specifically to avoid interference with the magnetic field and kept as thin as possible, it still causes a slight difference in tone, making the highs a bit rounder. However, this difference is barely noticeable and the cover protects the pickup from dirt, sweat and dust which, on an uncovered pickup, could get in the coils causing shorts.

So, even if many prefer the look of the uncovered pickup (especially if double whites or zebras) the cover can guarantee it a longer life.

As with original P 90s, P.A.F.s were not wax potted as butyrate bobbins can shrink considerably with the high temperatures necessary for the process. Today skilled winders can wax pot them on request, carefully using proprietary techniques to avoid any damage, but this should be done only if absolutely necessary, as potting effects tone. To avoid feedback it is very important for the assembly to be very sound so that nothing is allowed to vibrate.

Because of each of these factors, in all actuality, in every single example, even those sharing common tonal characters with others, each has its own unique personality.

Depending on the windings and the magnet grade used, some pickups from the same era can be quite bright, while others warm and fat, with many nuances from one extreme to the other. So it is quite impossible to characterize a "classic P.A.F. sound", but most experts agree that in general they have in common openness, organic feel and a broader dynamic range compared to most more modern pickups.

*Nickel silver baseplate, keeper, magnet, maple spacer, slug poles, bobbins, srew poles and the screws to secure the bobbins to the baseplate of a 1959 P.A.F.*

*P.A.F. pickup covers.*

*Springs, pickup mounting screws, pickup rings mounting screws.*

*Pickup rings from a 1959 ES 175D.*

# The Control Layout

The new humbucking pickup was connected to the usual control layout which represented the standard for Gibson. In two pickup models, there were individual volume and tone controls for each pickup. In the few models with three pickups, the middle one was engaged when the switch was in the middle position, where it functioned together with the bridge unit, sharing the same controls. On some Les Paul Customs the middle pickup was tied to the neck pickup and controls and usually one of the two pickups had a flipped magnet for an out-of-phase sound.

The potentiometers were all audio with a resistance of 500k and made by Centralab, but most read higher, some even above 600k. Until 1956 the capacitors were made by Cornell-Dubilier and nicknamed "Grey Tigers", and for a brief time some Mallory caps were used, but soon Gibson switched to Sprague "Bumblebee" caps. In 1960 white Astron caps were briefly used, and then again back to Sprague "Bumblebees" through the introduction of the SG shaped Les Pauls. Finally, by the end of 1961/early 1962, ceramic disks became the standard caps.

The circuit was a little different than in more recent guitars due to the way in which the capacitor was connected to the volume control. While in most modern guitars it is connected to the input lug of the volume pot, together with the lead from the pickup, in vintage guitars it was connected to the volume pot's output lug. This style of wiring is what is referred to as "50s wiring". With this layout of the controls, when turning down the volume the tone retains more high-end, so the sound cleans up without getting too muddy too soon.

The tone that made those guitars (Les Paul, ES 175, ES 335, ES 345, ES 355, Explorers, Flying V, ES 350, L-5 CES, Switchmaster) so desirable was not only due to the excellent pickups, but also to the transparent harnesses they were connected to, which allowed any nuance to be faithfully transferred to the amp. We should also credit the hardware used at the time. Gibson used Zamak bridges, with brass saddles, on brass posts (later switching to steel posts), lightweight aluminum 'stop' tailpieces on steel studs (see photo below). This combination, along with the Kluson tuning machines, kept the hardware light and able to transfer any and all tonal vibrations from the body and back to the strings for a very deep and transparent sound.

*1954 Les Paul Model*

*1954 Les Paul Model Junior*

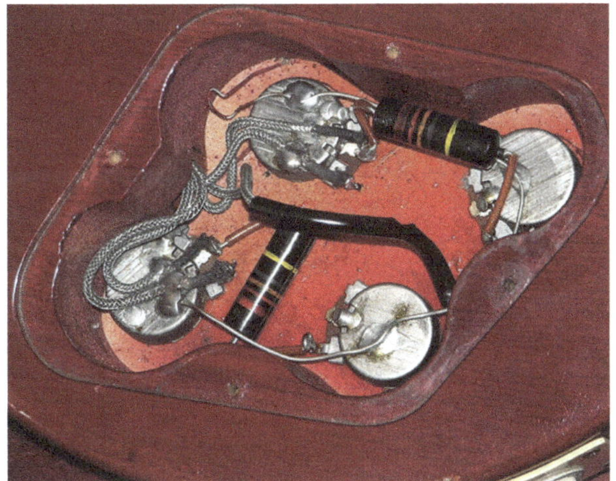

*1959 Les Paul Model*

*1960 Les Paul Standard*

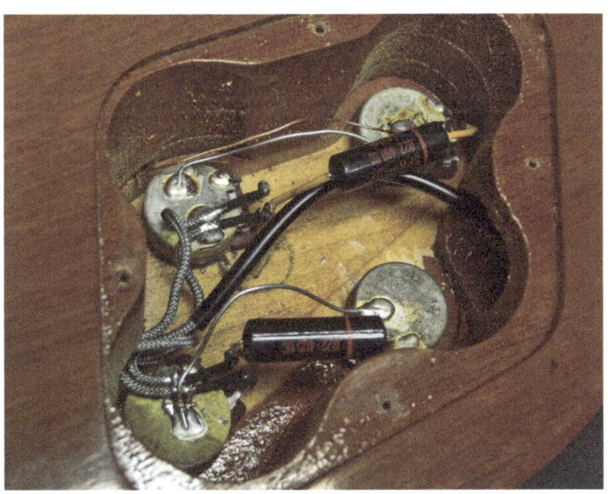

*1969 Les Paul Standard*

*Note the "Grey Tigers" used until 1956 and how the same components were used on the cheap Junior.*

*The "Bumblebee" caps became the stock items after 1956 but with some exceptions in 1960, when white Astron caps were used. When the Standard with two P 90s was reissued in 1969, it came with typical 1959 components, but the tone cap was connected to the input lug of the volume pot instead of the output as in the 1950s.*

# Inconsistencies In Old Pickups

In our computer age, the variances in resistance values, the use of magnets of different grades, make people say that the original humbucking pickup, like other models from that era, were inconsistent. We must remember that, at the time, the electric guitar was still relatively new; nobody knew how a pickup was supposed to be done or how it was supposed to sound. Gibson for sure was after a certain timbre that would set its instruments apart from those built by competitors, but as far as the average "Gibson tone" was achieved, that was fine, so they were chasing a sound accepting a certain tolerance on nuances, if a pickup came out a little brighter or warmer that wouldn't cause it to be rejected. They knew that they had to have a magnet of definite dimensions and to fill the bobbins enough; the technology of the time did not allow them to be too picky on details.

Says Aleksandar Vrhovec of Wizz pickups:

*In the fifties, they never compromised in the building of guitars or guitar parts. Everything was done a certain way for a good reason. I analyzed dozens of old pickups and I can honestly say I love them all. Vintage pickups were made with various steel alloys, various wire specifications, various grades of magnet and each one had different DC readings because they were wound just to fill the bobbins with wire. The bobbins were not wound to an exact number of turns, and considering that, every single vintage pickup is unique and desirable. For me, the perfect P.A.F. set must be clear, have depth, have vintage character, have control in the high end, smooth harmonic feedback, double tones, they must not be either too muddy or too sparkly, and must match well with the guitar's wood. I am always looking to get the sounds of Duane Allman, Billy Gibbons, Jimmy Page, Eric Clapton, etc. The list is long, but you get the idea. I always stick to replicating genuine old pickups the way they originally did it, and I don't care why they did something, I just do it the same way, because it is the only way to make them right. Of course maybe I am a little bit of a vintage correct freak, but there is no other way for me.*

The competition was fierce, Epiphone, before Gibson acquired the brand, was a strong competitor, Gretsch guitars were popular, and Fender was the new brand challenging everybody in the field. So saying that Gibson was concerned with quality is an understatement, as they were aiming at the professional market and so had to be the very best. When Gibson introduced the Les Paul Junior and the Special, even if they were designed for beginners, the quality had to be the same as for the fancier models, scrimping only on ornamentation and features. Even though the profit on those low-end models was relatively small, they were intended as instruments that would generate loyal customers, hopefully satisfied enough to upgrade to higher-end models as soon as they could afford to. Moreover, they did so well that several professionals used those "beginner" but terrific sounding guitars. Just think about the tone Leslie West was able to get with his Les Paul Junior!

At the same time Gibson never wasted money, so it was practical to save as much as possible, for example, using the same parts already in use for the P 90s, like the magnets and wire. As long as any pickup would fall in the range of what was considered a good "Gibson tone", it was fine, and if they were all a little different, each with its own character, this was not considered a negative thing, after all no two guitars sound exactly the same.

Not only was every single P.A.F. more or less different than the next one, but they were installed in different guitars, such as Les Pauls, ES 335s, ES 350s, ES 175s, and others. Listening to records made with them, that unmistakable "Gibson tone" is there and we tend to forget all about inconsistencies and individual specs.

# The End of the Golden Age

The end of 1956 introduced the humbucking model. During 1961 the M 55 magnet was replaced with the slightly shorter M 56, in AlNiCo 2 or AlNiCo 5 (as usual, long magnets still in stock continued to be used, so for a while some pickups could still have an M 55 magnet).

In 1962 Gibson reorganized the factory and moved the electronics department to a new area (Plant II). Around that time they started to put a label on the pickups with the number 2,737,842 (that is why they are called "Patent Number" pickups). Although, however, the 2,737,842 refers not to the patent for the humbucking pickup, but to the patent for the bridge/tailpiece used on 1952 Les Pauls. It is still unclear if that was done to deceive competitors, i.e., making it more difficult to find the real patent, or if it was a simple mistake.

At any rate, the pickups were identical no matter which label was used and were, in fact, used at random on the guitars, so that early sixties' instruments with both a P.A.F. and a Patent Number are not so rare.

At the time, new Meteor winding machines had been acquired and the windings on the pickups became more consistent, showing an average resistance of 7.3 kΩ -7.8kΩ with more balanced coils, but the occasional high wind pickup could still be found on some guitars as late as 1965.

During 1964, after a new reorganization responding to the increase in production that brought the electronics department to a new facility, the Plain Enamel wire was replaced with the less expensive (and easier to solder) Polyurethane insulation with a light copper color wire. This switch to a wire with different insulation, even if the gauge was still AWG 42, affected the tone of these pickups, and these Polywire pickups have their own character indeed, which is quite different from that of the PE wire pickups.

As always, Gibson would use whatever was still in stock, so, for a while, pickups wound with plain enamel wire could occasionally be found on guitars from that era.

# 1960's Pre-T-Top P.A.F. Bobbin Patent Number Decal Pickup Repair

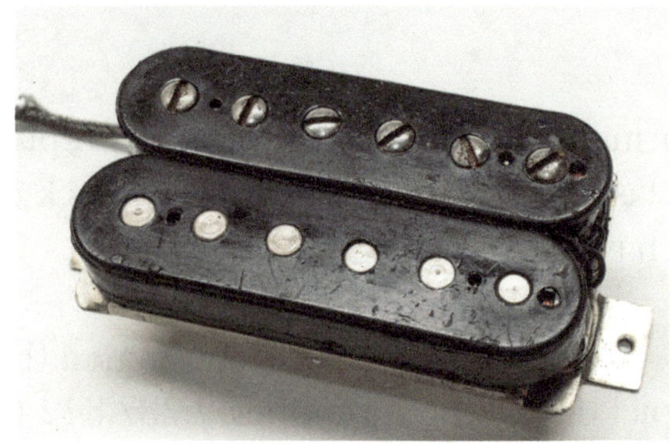

*Pre-T-Top view and bottom view.*

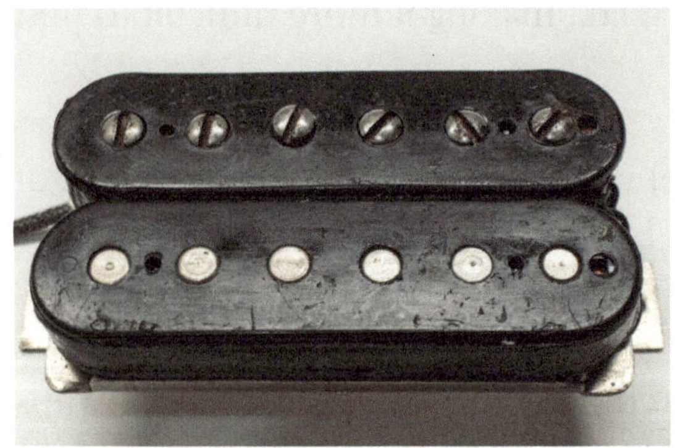

*... top view, showing uniquenesses in slugs, differences in bobbin windows, and "mold #4" light circle mark on left side of slug bobbin.*

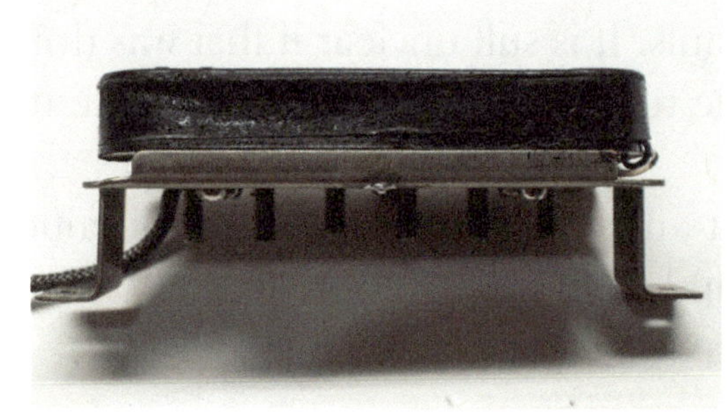

*... side view, showing original slug coil taping.*

*...other side view, showing original screw coil taping. Note the hand-torn tape and missing hookup lead connection tape mark.*

*... distinctive "L" marks on foot.*

*... another view of the "L" marks and the non-typical bobbin mounting screws.*

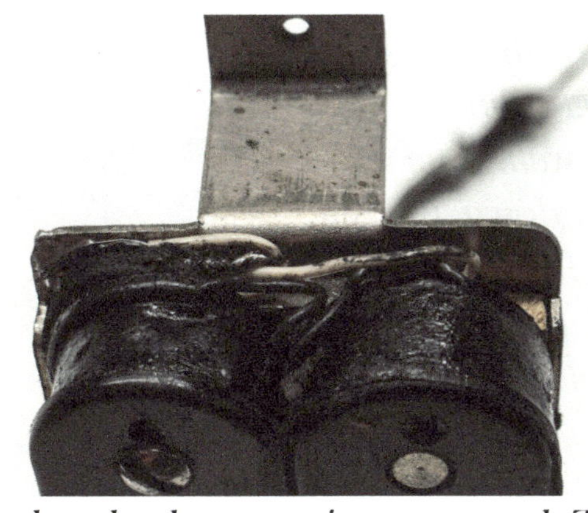

*...hookup lead connections exposed. The original tape covering this area has fallen away over time. Note that it is the coil starts, rather than the finishes, which are the white leads, in this case.*

*... the other side of the humbucker, showing the original loose coil taping and exposed magnet end. A blob of solder can be seen on the hookup lead near the baseplate, which may indicate the original position and type of guitar this pickup was removed from. Some guitar designs had the string ground wire connected to the bridge pickup lead at this point.*

*...slug coil removed from baseplate, exposing a heavily processed cast magnet and a very straight grain maple spacer.*

*... slug coil removed from baseplate, showing the underside of the slug bobbin and the North side indicating mark on the magnet.*

*...magnet removed, this rough cast magnet had to be ground heavily on all sides to bring it to the correct size. Though this looks like a modern polished magnet, in many ways, it is original to the pickup and this practice of grinding to spec was common, though not often to this extent.*

*...underside of the removed magnet, showing more processing on the underside.*

*... end view of magnet. Even the ends of this magnet were ground flat to bring the magnet into size spec.*

*...opposite end view of magnet, showing more evidence of grinding on this surface, as well. The black lines going down the side are marks from where the loosely wrapped coil tape was trapped under the bobbins. These will serve as an indicator of the top surface when reinstalling the magnet.*

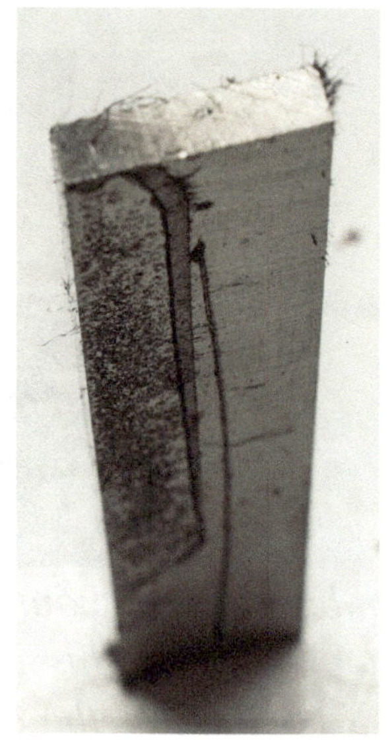

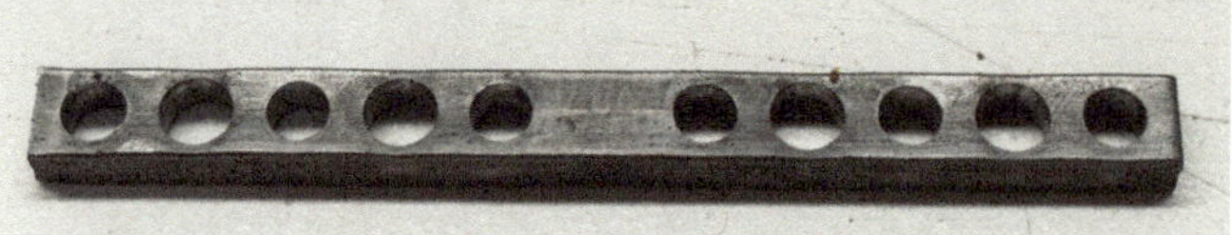

...keeper bar removed. Note the later-style steel keeper bar, easily identified by the somewhat warped and wobbly surfaces which are perfectly flat on earlier machined keeper bars present in P.A.F.s and earlier P 90s.

*... original slug coil with coil tape removed.*

*...bobbin mounting screws sitting very close to the fully charged magnet. Note that these unusual screws, though silver in color, are not magnetic steel, as is sometimes the case. These do not appear to be plated brass, and may be stainless steel. The shape is exactly the same as what is seen in brass P.A.F. bobbin mounting screws.*

*...original screw coil with coil tape removed.*

*...slugs removed, top view. Note the uniqueness of each one in the cutoff marks and chamfering.*

*...slugs removed, side view. This view shows well the great differences in chamfering, from one to the next, as well as the cutoff tooling marks.*

*The rarely seen insides of P.A.F. bobbins. As was known from the light circle mark at the end of the slug bobbin, the inside markings confirm that this is a "mold #4" bobbin. The screw bobbin is a "mold #1" bobbin. Also, note the differences in font size and shape used for the inside markings of these bobbins.*

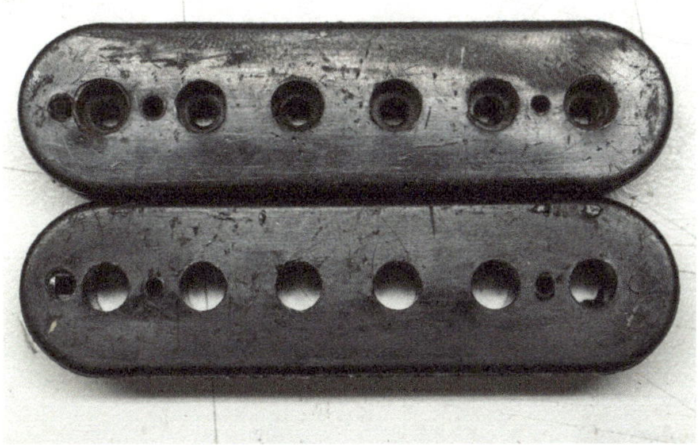

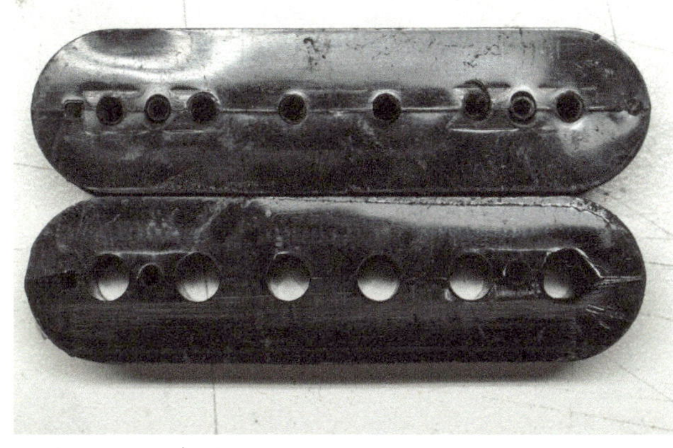

*...top view of stripped bobbins, and underside view of stripped bobbins. The seams, running left to right, can be seen here, as well as the impressions left from the keeper bar and magnet. The plastic, on the right underside of the slug bobbin, around the final slug is starting to peel off and flake away.*

*... reassembled humbucker. The coils were re-wound with plain enamel wire, more appropriate for earlier P.A.F.s, at the request of the customer, in this case.*

*... this view shows the unique "square in a circle" bobbin windows on the screw and slug coil. Also shown are the rare non-brass tips of the bobbin mounting screws.*

In 1965 another change took place, the bobbins no longer had the distinctive square hole in a ring as found on earlier versions, but instead had a "T" embossed on top and later, around 1967, the material was also changed from butyrate to ABS. According to some experts, the different bobbins also affected tone, as the ABS bobbins had slightly different inner dimensions, making for a change in winding parameters, thus giving the T-Top models an audibly different tonal character than previous Patent Number pickups, even if the wire used was the same.

To many this was the end of the golden era for the Gibson humbucking pickup.

*1966 ES 335TD. A strong favorite among musicians of different styles, especially studio session players, this model remaind succesful through the decades, even during Gibson's darkest times.*

# 1960's Patent Decal T-Top

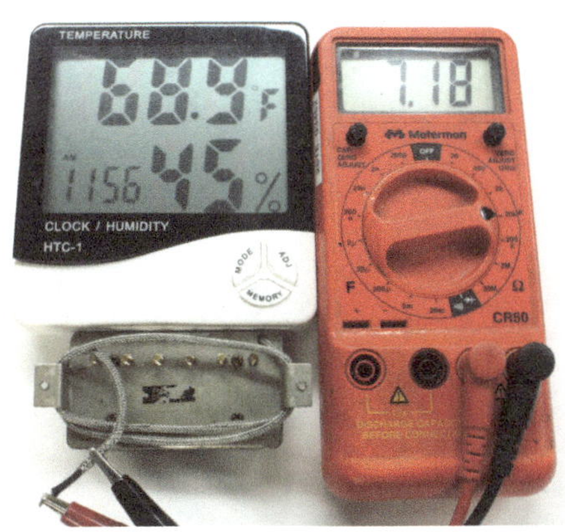


*Typical DCR reading of an early T-Top. By this time in Gibson's pickup production, coil production had become much more consistent from one to the next than in previous years.*

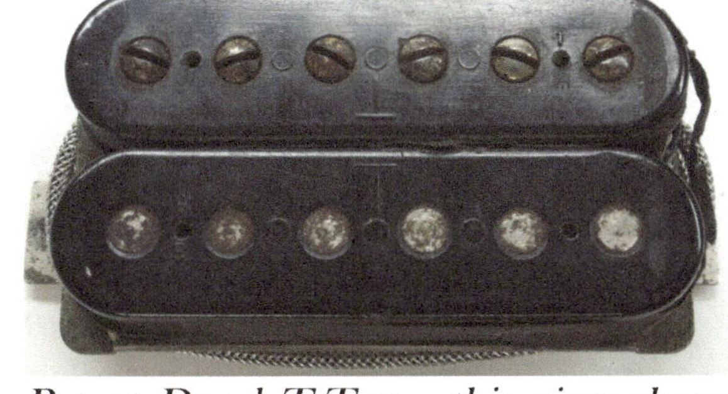

*Patent Decal T-Top , this view shows the "T" markings on the bobbin tops, presumably built into the molds to indicate the top side of the bobbins to simplify pickup assembly. These marks are where the "T-Top" name comes from.*

*Underside view, showing the remains of the patent number decal, the brass Phillips screws, and the "L" marks on the feet. Note that original hookup lead was replaced before taking this photo.*

*Closeup of the patent number decal. Note the clean underside of the gold plated pole screws.*

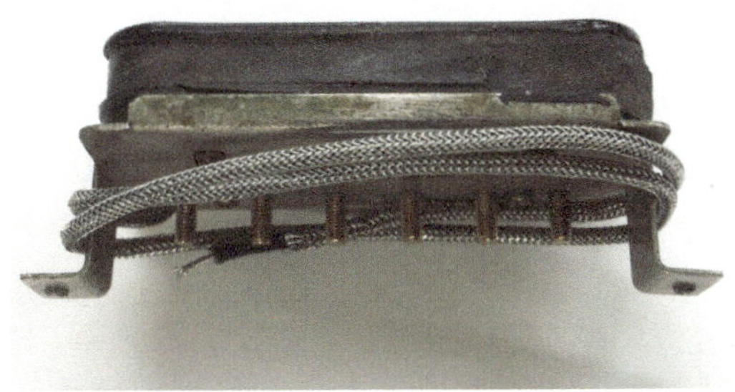

*Side view, showing the original taping of the slug coil and hookup lead connections.*

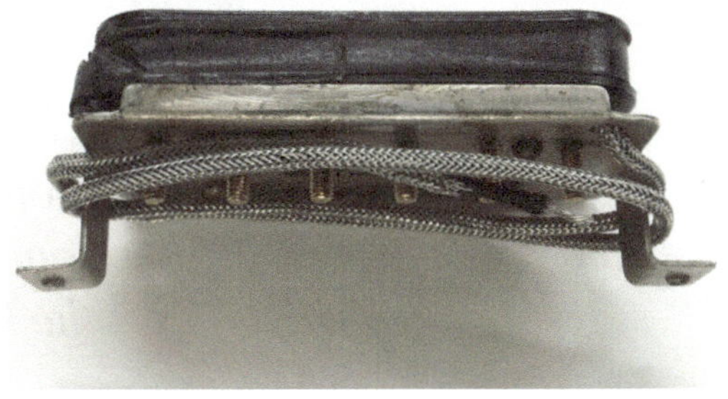

*Other side view, showing the original taping of the screw coil and hookup lead connections.*

*Closeup of the brass bobbin mounting screws and solder splatter on the baseplate. In this photo, the threading for the pole screws in the baseplate can be clearly seen around the gold plated pole screws.*

*Closeup of the underside of this pickup. The looser baseplate threading can be seen around the gold plated pole screw in the bottom left of the image. The raised gold lettering over the black enamel background of the patent number decal is also evident.*

*Showing the "L" tooling marks of the baseplate foot.*

*Alternate view of the baseplate foot. This images shows the de-burring around the edges of the foot.*

*Another view of the foot, showing the depth of the "L" marks in the baseplate material, which is shallower than some others.*

*Straight-on view of the foot, showing the "L" marks. In some photos, "L" marks can seem to disappear but from the right angles or at a close view they are present.*

*Alternate straight-on view of the foot, showing the cleaned-up, somewhat rounded over edges of the foot.*

*Another view of the foot, showing how the "L" marks can change and nearly disappear with different lighting and angles.*

*Closeup of the slug bobbin top, showing the "T" and other mold markings on the bobbin surface. The rings around the slug holes may have been to help guide the insertion of the slugs.*

*Closeup of the screw bobbin top. The plating is both wearing through and flaking off of the screws from use and oxidization. The bobbin manufacturer's mold marking is also present below the "1" and the bobbin mounting screw hole.*

*Showing the hookup lead connections. Note that the coil finishes, not the starts, are white in these later model humbuckers.*

*View of the dried out and decaying paper tape covering the hookup lead connections.*

*Side view of pickup, showing the braided shield hookup entry point, the side of the magnet, keeper bar, maple spacer and the paper taped coils. At the very top of the slug bobbin, a small amount of the bright red poly wire can be seen peeking through a crack in the coil tape.*

*Closeup view of the slug coil showing the bright red poly wire, used in these post-P.A.F. humbuckers, through a small crack in the paper coil tape.*

# From Going Far From The Original To A Slight Return

Gibson, in 1972, equipped the SG Standard and Custom with new, Bill Lawrence designed high output pickups called the "Super Humbucking" model, with ceramic magnets and, for the first time, with different specs for the neck and bridge positions. Bill Lawrence designed other pickups for Gibson such as "The Original" and a special version of the Super Humbucking pickup used on the L6-S guitars (which was also sold as an aftermarket item called the 'True Blues').

In the eighties came Tim Shaw, designer of the 'Velvet Brick Model', who got the go ahead to resume some of the original "Patent Applied For" pickup specs for the "Pat. Appl. For" model used on the Heritage Les Paul series and some early Reissues. In the nineties, in an attempt to offer different versions of the original humbucking pickup, a new model was introduced as the '57 Classic' (a P.A.F. Reissue), which was followed by the Burstbucker series and the more recent Custom Buckers.

# The Brothers Of The P.A.F. Model

When Gibson acquired Epiphone in 1957, a new pickup was designed for the high-end guitar models, while the others were fitted with P 90 pickups. The new pickup was humbucking, but to differentiate it from the Gibson model and to make it fit with the cavities cut for the original "New York" Epiphone single coil pickups, it was smaller, with thin nylon bobbins and, because of the reduced available space, less turns of the same wire used on the Gibson pickup. The average DC resistance was about 7kΩ and the sound was slightly thinner and brighter than the regular humbucker. This miniaturized version of the humbucking pickup had the same "Patent Applied For" label and underwent the same changes occurring on the bigger model. So it got a "Patent Number" label in 1962 and the wire was changed from Plain Enamel to Poly in 1964.

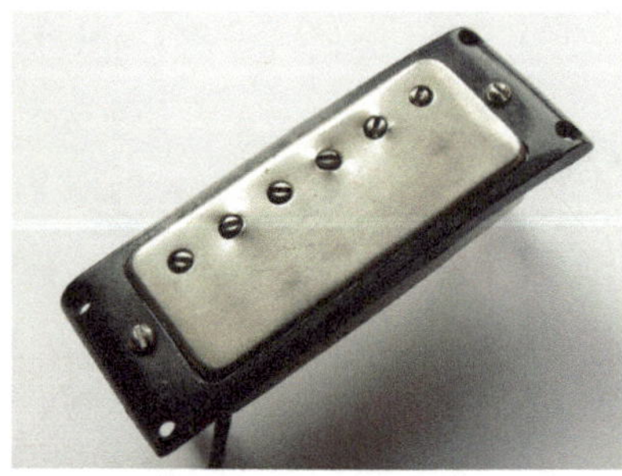

*Gibson Mini Humbucking pickup.*

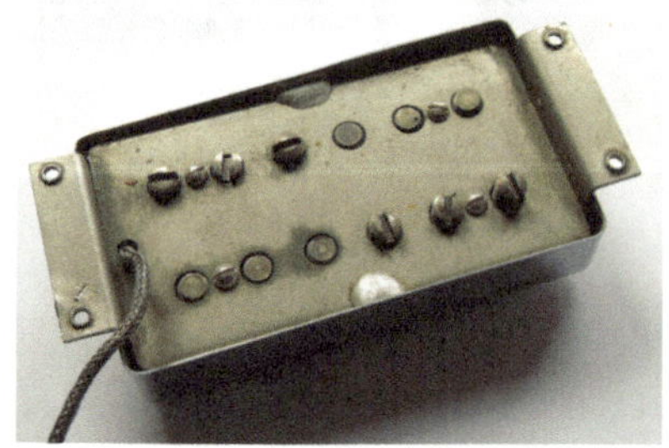

*Fender 1972 Humbucking pickup designed by Seth Lover.*

When the Les Paul Deluxe was introduced in 1969, replacing the previous year's Standard and fit ted with P 90 pickups, Gibson used mini-humbucking pickups, similar to the late sixties Epiphone version, installed with modified P 90 covers in order to avoid having to cut new cavities in the guitars.

A similar version was fitted to the Johnny Smith guitar, differentiated by a magnet inserted in one bobbin instead of the usual slug pole pieces, and a ferrous plate which transferred the magnetic field to the pole pieces in the other coil.

When the Firebird Series was introduced in 1963, yet another model was designed for those guitars. It had the same structure as the Epiphone model, but instead of miniaturized pole pieces, it had two small bar magnets inside the bobbins, for a punchier sound, and a cover without holes. The earlier units had Plain Enamel wire, while since 1964, even on those, the Poly wire was used, and the tone became thinner and even somewhat harsh.

*Early fifties Epiphone Zephyr Deluxe Regent with "NewYork" single coil pickups.*

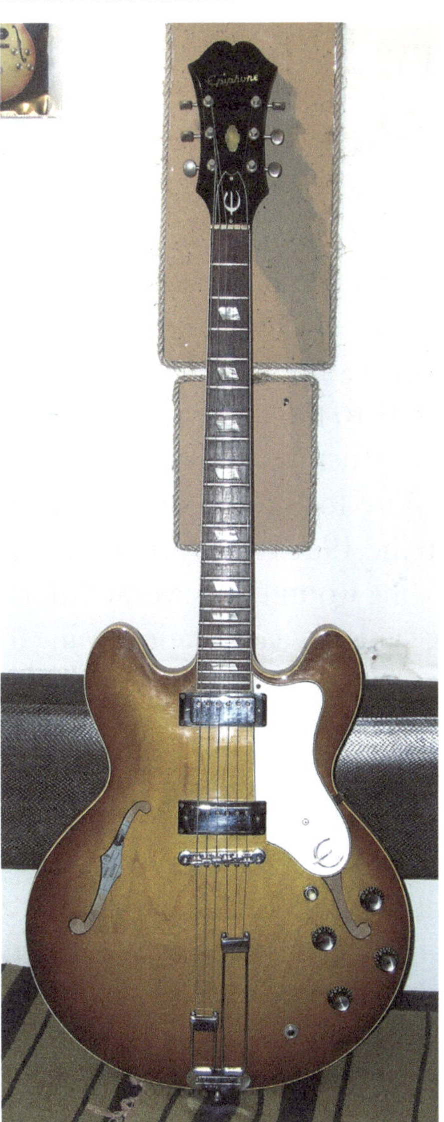

*1964 Epiphone Riviera with Gibson Mini humbucking pickups.*

*1963 Gibson Firebird V with proprietary Mini humbucking pickups.*

Since Gibson made pickups for other manufacturers as well, another version was built for Silvertone which had three adjustable pole pieces on the bobbin facing the neck on the bass side, and three on the other bobbin under the treble strings. Except for the pole piece arrangement, those were the same as the Epiphone units (Seth Lover used the same pole piece arrangement when he designed the bigger humbucking model for Fender which was later known as the 'Wide Range' humbucker, but in that case they were in fact Cunife magnets shaped as screws).

The various types of mini-humbucking models have a bad reputation for a harsh tone and for being too prone to feedback. However, the pre-64 models, with Plain Enamel wire in the coils, share many of the qualities of P.A.F. and "Patent Number" models from the same era, with just a slightly thinner and brighter tone, but still with plenty of warmth. In reality they are quite similar, but with a little less punch and a little more definition.

# The Lust For Airy Fatness, The Many But Related Voices Of P.A.F. Pickups

Though the elusive "P.A.F.-tone" may be nonexistent as a singular voice, these bold and beautifully voiced pickups do share some commonalities in sonic structure throughout their entire product range. Much is talked about regarding the physical differences in P.A.F.s and how they translate to tonal differences from one P.A.F. to the next, and sometimes the similarities are forgotten. It is true that steel parts varied a bit in structure, composition and physical shape while magnet types, sizes and charges also differed. Wire tolerances such as wire core thickness, insulation thickness and ohms-per-foot were looser in the 1950s and varied more than today. Different coil patterns on P.A.F.s exist as a result of coils being wound on several different winding machines, many of these machines having several winding stations, each station using a unique spool of wire and particular tension and setup. P.A.F. coils were paired up with one another in a humbucker with no regard for electrical or sonic characteristics, significantly increasing the differences from one P.A.F. set to the next. Even the wire routing and coil taping technique varied a little bit during the golden era of Seth Lover's P.A.F. at Ted McCarty's Gibson, and there is surely at least someone who deeply believes that those variances change something ever so slighty, yet importantly, about the sound of a P.A.F. It is necessary to acknowledge all the differences in design, composition and processing that occurred in production during the best years of bucked hum. Still, we see some less often discussed, but commonly agreed as desirable, sonic qualities that are common to nearly all P.A.F.s from the first ones installed in 1957 right up through the end of P.A.F. production in the 1960s.

There is a combination of fullness and clarity, common to P.A.F.s. Whether a lower output A5 P.A.F. with a tight low end and bright jangle, or warm and saturated A2 P.A.F. with hot coils. There invariably seem to be some common sonic qualities that all P.A.F.s share: a full, present and detailed low end and, simultaneously, a clear, breathy, open airiness in the very extended top end.

P.A.F.s can sound brighter and chirpier, cleaner, dynamic and more accurate, thicker and more vocal, or much warmer or even darker than each other. Many later P.A.F.s have a lower output with a slightly metallic, almost liquid chirp on the top end and others have a thick, vocal growl with more compression and harmonics in the midrange from the coils. Consistently, it seems, P.A.F.s all have "bigger," and yet also somehow at the same time, "cleaner" qualities to their voices. There is a fatness with an airy top end. Using various words to describe the same thing, people often talk about these desirable qualities of P.A.F.s. Even the warmest and darkest examples are typically complemented with greater clarity across the board, i.e., an open and detailed top end and a more dynamic output than one would ever expect for such a boldly voiced pickup. In pickups, there is usually a tradeoff between where a pickup can lean towards either a big, fat harmonically rich and aggressive sound or a pretty and breathy clean sound. More of one will usually take something away from the other. However, P.A.F.s seem to do it all at the same time.

*As long as I've been exposed to P.A.F.s in my life I've always found the full, bold, richness combined with the open, breathy top end is what makes real golden-age P.A.F.s stand out uniquely from all other similarly designed pickups, old and new. Capturing that "having both extremes at the same time" in a humbucker is what first drove me to attempt to build a better reproduction of that amazing humbucker sound. Having success in achieving that is what continues to drive me to produce more great versions of the many various voicings of the original P.A.F.s. This "airy fatness" is the common ground of P.A.F.s.*
James Finnerty, ReWind Electric, LLC

*1959 Gibson Les Paul Model.*

# Classic Tones

P.A.F. equipped guitars have been used by players in a wide range of musical styles since they appeared, and can be heard in recordings from Joe Pass, Wes Montgomery, Chuck Berry, Albert King, and many others. Nonetheless, not everybody preferred the new model. Among jazz players the old "Charlie Christian" straight-bar pickup was still popular, so much so that Gibson continued to make it available upon request.

In his 1967 book "The Guitar", in the chapter on guitar pickups, Barney Kessel was still advocating usage of the "Charlie Christian". Here he writes: "I advise the use of the straight-bar type when you wish a rich, lush sound. With this pickup you are less aware of amplification, and achieve a more natural, woody guitar sound, but with more volume." About the "Charlie Christian" he further added that: "It is best used in jazz, dance bands, and wherever you are required to produce great guitar tone quality". Kessel admitted, most likely with regard to the P 90, that: "The screw type of pickup makes it easier to achieve string balance through the adjustment of six screws which are in the magnetic pickup and placed under each string". However, again in reference to the P 90, he also stated that: "Compared to the straight-bar, this pickup produces more highs and a thinner, more nasal sound", and that it is preferable "wherever a gimmick sound is needed".

Relatively clean guitar sounds still dominated rock and roll in the early sixties, and even if players like Pat Hare, Hubert Sumlin, and Link Wray had experimented with distortion during the previous decade, it was in the United Kingdom, that it became a bona fide style. Ultimately, the Les Paul was found to be the guitar best suited for that sound.

During a tour in the United States in May of 1965 the British rock band, The Rolling Stones, recorded a song called "(I Can't Get No) Satisfaction". The song was released a month later as a single. Keith Richards played the main riff using a Firebird VII along with a Gibson made Maestro Fuzztone and a Fender amp (Richards at the time favored a Fender Showman). The song became a worldwide hit and people began noticing Richards' choice of instruments. Even if a Firebird was used on the recording, when the Stones played the song on television, Richards, probably one of the first famous players to buy a Burst, showed up with his '59 Bigsby equipped Gibson Les Paul. That is what people saw and that is what they immediately desired.

Eric Clapton bought his first Gibson guitar, an ES 335 TD, in 1964. It was rumored to have a pair of leftover P.A.F.s, stock from the factory, instead of the usual "Patent Number" pickups of the day. However, after seeing the album cover of Freddie King's "Let's Hide Away And Dance Away", on which the bluesman is holding a Gold Top Les Paul, Clapton decided he had to have one of those.

Clapton could not find a Gold Top Les Paul in London, so, in June 1965 he bought a second hand Sunburst Les Paul. In early 1966 that was the guitar used to record John Mayall's album "Blues Breakers with Eric Clapton" and the world was exposed to the wailing sustain and the broad range of tones that could only be achieved with a P.A.F. loaded Les Paul through a cranked Marshall combo amplifier.

After leaving John Mayall & the Bluesbreakers, Clapton, then with Cream, used a P.A.F. equipped

Les Paul Sunburst, a P.A.F. equipped Les Paul Custom, a "Patent Number" equipped SG Standard, his ES 335 TD and a mini-humbucking equipped Firebird 1. Through these he delivered his famous "woman tone", achieved by turning down the guitar's tone control while turning up the volume of his 100 watt Marshalls as heard on "Fresh Cream", "Disraeli Gears", and "Wheels Of Fire".

When Clapton left the Bluesbreakers his replacement was Peter Green, who in October 1966 also used a Les Paul/Marshall combination for the recording of "A Hard Road".
Green continued to deliver clear but driving tones with the Fleetwood Mac as heard on "Peter Green's Fleetwood Mac", "Mr. Wonderful", "The Pious Bird of Good Omen", and "Blues Jam in Chicago".
Following in the steps of Eric Clapton and Peter Green was not easy, but Mayall always had a good ear for guitar players and he was impressed by a 17-year-old Mick Taylor. In 1967 Taylor recorded "Crusade" with Mayall, then his Les Paul was stolen and he bought Keith Richards' Bigsby equipped Les Paul, which was used on several Stones hits. Mayall remembers that Mick's development as a lead player was very fast and soon the band's concerts were crowded by other guitar players in awe of the new Bluesbreaker as heard on "Diary of a Band". With ex-Richards' '59 Les Paul and a 50 watt Marshall head with 4x12 cabs, Taylor played on other Mayall albums, such as "Blues From Laurel Canyon" and "Bare Wires", both released in 1968.
After Taylor left the Bluesbreakers he added his fantastic vibrato and slide prowess to the music of the Rolling Stones. Taylor played his Burst along with other guitars, such as a Les Paul/SG, an ES 345 and a 1969 ES 355 (most noted for the solo in "Can't You Hear Me Knocking") on albums like "Sticky Fingers", "Get Yer Ya-Ya's Out", "Exile On Main Street", "Goats Head Soup", and "It's Only Rock & Roll". Alongside Taylor, Keith Richards delivered nasty leads and driving riffs using a wide assortment of guitars including a Les Paul Sunburst, Les Paul Junior, Les Paul Custom and a Gibson Flying V.

A young session player of the time, Jimmy Page, used a Les Paul Custom in the studio, switching to a Fender Telecaster for the first album of his band, the Led Zeppelin. Ultimately, even if he used other guitars, from a Danelectro to a Stratocaster, his carefully orchestrated guitar parts were achieved mostly with a Sunburst Les Paul on the albums "II", "III", "IV", "Houses of the Holy", and "Physical Graffiti".

Paul Kossoff with The Free, Steve Hackett with Genesis, Clem Clemson with Colosseum, and Tony McPhee with The Groundhogs (SG/Les Paul) were all playing P.A.F. equipped Les Pauls; and the list goes on.

In the USA the most influential player was Michael Bloomfield, the hottest guitar player in Chicago. After the album "East-West" was issued in 1966, on which he played a 1956 Gold Top Les Paul with P 90 pickups, Bloomfield left the Paul Butterfield Blues Band to form the Electric Flag and in 1968 used a 1959 Sunburst Les Paul to record "A Long Time Coming". Players took notice and the guitar of choice became a Sunburst Les Paul, especially after Bloomfield appeared with it on the cover of the 1968 album "Super Session".

Bloomfield favored Fender amps and sparkly clean tones and the degree to which how expressive a Les Paul can sound with those 6L6 powered amps is clearly demonstrated on the great album "Live at Bill Graham's Fillmore West 1969".

In 1969, the Allman Brothers Band was formed, and on their first album Duane Allman and Dickey Betts used, respectively, a Gibson ES 335 and an ES 345. While Allman had his Gold Top Les Paul in the studio, and Betts his Les Paul SG, they were not used on the recordings and became their guitars of choice shortly afterward.

Complementing "Brownie", Eric Clapton's 1956 Fender Stratocaster, Allman used his P.A.F. equipped Gold Top Les Paul on Clapton's post-Cream release "Layla and Other Assorted Love Songs" which was released in November of 1970. This was the only studio album from Derek & the Dominos and is often cited as Clapton's greatest musical accomplishment. Just toward the end of the recording of the "Layla" album, in September 1970, Duane Allman traded his Gold Top Les Paul with Stone Balloon's guitarist Rick Stine for a Cherry Sunburst Les Paul. Since he preferred the tone of the Gold Top's 1957 P.A.F. pickups part of the deal was that the guitars would have them swapped. That Cherry Les Paul with the Gold Top's pickups is the guitar heard on the immortal March 1971 Fillmore Concerts.

The Allman Brothers got fat sounds from P.A.F.s and Marshall Amps as testified to on "At Fillmore East" which is often cited as the best live album ever produced. Studio albums featuring the Allman Cherry Burst Les Paul with Gold Top P.A.F.s and Darkburst Les Paul a.k.a. "Hot 'Lanta" include "Idlewild South" and "Eat a Peach".

*1960 Gibson Les Paul Standard. In that year, Gibson used for the first time the name Standard in that catalogue, and also revised the finish with a new formula for the red so that it would not fade as before.*

There has always been a bit of confusion about Duane Allman's two P.A.F. loaded bursts, so to clarify, it was the Cherry Burst which was used on "At Fillmore East" and it did not have very hot pickups (both the bridge and neck measured about 7kΩ). The P.A.F.s in the Cherry Burst were the 'Layla Pickups' and were removed from Allman's 1957 Gold Top. Hot 'Lanta was NOT used on "At Fillmore East". This Darkburst Les Paul was purchased in June of 1971 and had very 'hot' pickups (measuring 8.7kΩ in the bridge and 8.3kΩ in the neck). These pickups originally came from the factory installed in the opposite positions, but had been switched over before Duane got the guitar. Both sets of P.A.F.s sounded mighty fine in the hands of a true guitar legend.

Players from both sides of the Atlantic suddenly started looking for humbucking equipped Gibson guitars. This sudden attention is not surprising, as the classic P.A.F. tone was pretty much the same as the signature tone Gibson established with the P 90, albeit somewhat smoother. The lack of noise allowed players to use the humbucking pickup at very high volumes without hum interference while allowing for incredible sustain and a very broad dynamic range.

While Jimi Hendrix and Rory Gallagher remained faithful to the Fender Stratocaster, making it the quintessential electric guitar in the late sixties, in the early seventies, humbucking equipped guitars ruled. From the ES 335 used by Alvin Lee to the ES 345 favored by Freddy King and Elvin Bishop, and the ES 355 TD-SV used by B.B. King, Jimmy Dawkins and other bluesmen, the P.A.F. reigned supreme.

Grace Slick's music was driven by Jorma Kaukonen's ES 345 in the Jefferson Airplane and later by Craig Chaquico's Les Paul in the Jefferson Starship.

In California, for some reason, the SG was more popular. On the Quicksilver Messenger Service live album "Happy Trails, which was recorded from two live performances at the Fillmore East and Fillmore West, John Cipollina's guitar work made "Who Do You Love" one of the most popular rock and roll recordings to come out of San Francisco.

Gibson SG Standard wielding Barry "the Fish" Melton of Country Joe & The Fish and dual SG wielders Sam Andrew and James Gurley of Janis Joplin's band Big Brother and the Holding Company helped to establish the SG Standard as Gibson's best-selling model of all time.

Country influenced rock bands like the Charlie Daniels Band, Gary Rossington's Lynyrd Skynyrd and Toy Caldwell's Marshall Tucker Band, among many others, used P.A.F. loaded Les Pauls. Marshall Tucker's double album "Where We All Belong" shows them at their best in the studio and live while demonstrating, yet again, the versatility of P.A.F. humbucking pickups.
From Texas came the attention grabbing tones of Billy Gibbons' Les Paul, nicknamed "Pearly Gates", with ZZ Top. Their best-known album being "Tres Hombres", with some of the finest guitar tones ever recorded.

Even Jeff Beck, for some time favored a Les Paul for the thick tones on the album "Truth" with Rod Stewart on vocals, then went back to the Stratocaster and back again to an Oxblood refinished early fifties Les Paul outfitted with two P.A.F. pickups for his solo album "Wired".

*Classic tones and looks: Double cream P.A.F.s and flame top.*

This was the era now remembered as the "classic rock" era and in these albums are the "classic sounds" representing it. This era is still influential and inspired more modern players like Gary Moore, who often used Peter Green's Les Paul, which he bought after the ex-Fleetwood Mac/ex-Bluesbreaker player suffered a breakdown and got fed up with the music business. Robben Ford, Slash, Mark Knopfler, Warren Haynes, Larry Carlton, Ace Frehley, Joe Perry, Zakk Wylde, Peter Frampton, Warren Haynes, Neal Schon, Derek Trucks, Greg Martin, Joe Bonamassa, J. D. Simo, Steve Jones and countless others are still making splendid use of P.A.F. equipped Gibson guitars.

*1959 Gibson Les Paul Model.*

# The P.A.F. Legacy
## Old Sounds For Modern Players

Tone has always been important to musicians, but until what was later to become known as the "British Invasion", it was not overly emphasized. While before this "assault" everyone could tell Wes Montgomery from Barney Kessel by their tones (as well as their playing style) however, the attention paid to their gear was relatively limited. Probably Eric Clapton in the UK and Michael Bloomfield in the USA changed the way fans looked at the instruments in use.

Even before the "British Invasion" players wanted to play like their heroes, sax players were seeking the tones of Lester Young and Charlie Parker and guitar players were chasing the tones of Charlie Christian and Kenny Burrell. However, when Clapton and Bloomfield made the electric guitar the main instrument of the band and gave it a hitherto unknown popularity, suddenly every component of their heroes rig was being scrutinized with unprecedented attention. Not only did players want to sound like their idols, but they wanted to have the same instruments, the only ones that were reputedly good enough for the job.

When Bloomfield played a Fender Telecaster that was the right guitar, then he switched to a Gold Top P 90 equipped Les Paul sales of that model sky rocketed. When he switched again, to a Sunburst Les Paul, everything else was deemed inferior. To accentuate this idea, other famous players such as Peter Green, Mick Taylor, Paul Kossoff, Jimmy Page and Duane Allman all played Sunburst Les Pauls. Clapton and others also played SGs and ES 335s, but as far as people were concerned "the" tone was a Gibson guitar with P.A.F. pickups played through a Marshall amp.

This was the myth, although in reality, Marshalls were not the only amps being used as Ampeg, Orange and Hiwatt were also quite popular. However, the Les Paul/Marshall combination was synonymous with a humbucking equipped Gibson guitar in conjunction with any powerful amp, just as any electric bass, regardless of the brand, was generically referred to as a "Fender" bass. Moreover, in all honesty, some "typical" tones were not even made with humbucking pickups.

The problem was that, since 1960, Gibson was not producing any more Les Pauls and recent SGs and ES 335s had pickups which weren't even remotely sonically close to the old "Patent Applied For" pickups.

In 1968 Gibson reintroduced two Les Paul models, a Standard and a Custom. However, the Standard was only offered with a gold top and two P 90 pickups while the Custom had a maple top and two "T-Top" humbucking pickups. In 1969 the Standard was "upgraded" with mini humbucking pickups and a new name: Deluxe. In 1974, finally, a new Standard was introduced, but it was still quite different from the original and had the same "T-Top" pickups as the Custom. At that time the Custom was no longer made with a solid mahogany body, but had a maple cap just like the Standard and the only differences were the ebony fretboard, the finish and the gold hardware. Also

*In 1968 Gibson reintroduced the Les Paul Standard, but with a gold top and P 90 pickups, in 1969 replaced the pickups with mini humbuckers and renamed it Deluxe, but they were not exactly what players were asking for.*

gone was the sometimes richly figured two-piece maple top of the original Standard, replaced by a plain three-piece top with a back constructed of laminated woods.

Eric Clapton encouraged young players to buy used guitars as they were made better, and the hunt for original Les Pauls was on.

Some rock players seemed quite happy with their new guitars and Michael Shenker of the Scorpions, Randy Rhoads of Quiet Riot (and later with Ozzy Osbourne), Lindsey Buckingham of Fleetwood Mac, Mick Ronson with David Bowie, and many others got great distorted and clean tones from T-Top loaded Norlin era guitars. In 1972, when the original P.A.F. in his Les Paul broke, Jimmy Page replaced the bridge pickup on his "Number 1" guitar with a T-Top and of course made the resulting P.A.F./T-Top combination another favorite among his many devoted followers. Larry Carlton became a legendary session man using a late-sixties ES 335 loaded with stock "Patent Number" pickups.

Others, however, like Dickey Betts, Charlie Daniels, Billy Gibbons, Joe Walsh, Don Felder with the Eagles, Gary Rossington with Lynyrd Skynyrd and many others, were playing P.A.F. loaded Les Pauls and explaining through the pages of Guitar Player magazine how old guitars were better made, had better feel and better tones than anything being made at the time. Even Carlos Santana, when he switched from Gibson to Paul Reed Smith guitars, had P.A.F. pickups installed on his instruments.

In the meantime rock music grew heavier and players seemed to fall into two different camps: those looking for those old guitars which were reputed as better suited to blues based rock, and those seeking more distortion and thus more powerful pickups to get more saturated tones from the relatively low gain amps of the time. Since the late sixties a few talented guys were already winding pickups for professional players. Seymour Duncan, worked for the likes of Jeff Beck, Jimi Hendrix and others. David Schecter, was winding high output pickups for session men in California. Also, Dan Armstrong, was building high output pickups with powerful ceramic magnets for the Ampeg Lucite (clear plastic) guitars. However, for the average player who could not find or afford a vintage guitar and/or wanted new pickups for his recent model, there was nothing available on the market. A solution for them came from Larry DiMarzio.

*Les Paul Deluxe*

DiMarzio introduced the Super Distortion pickup in 1972, a model promising thick and loud tones thanks to overwound coils and a powerful ceramic magnet. For the more traditional players (or for the neck slot when paired with a Super Distortion in the bridge), DiMarzio introduced the P.A.F. Model in 1974. The name notwithstanding, the DiMarzio P.A.F. was not a faithful copy of the original Gibson humbucker, but rather a revised version of the Gibson models of the time, with an M 55 sized AlNiCo 5 magnet and Teflon wire. Regardless, DiMarzio received a trademark for the name of the new model as well as for the color of the uncovered cream bobbins. DiMarzio also offered Fender style models and other replacement parts to customize guitars.

The combination of the idea that players could modify their guitars and make them sound closer to their liking, along with DiMarzio's success, opened the door for a whole new industry. Soon, other companies, such as Mighty Mite and Schecter, were offering pickups and replacement parts to the point that the adventurous player could assemble a whole guitar with bodies, necks, tuners, pots and pickups of his or her choice. At the time most builders did not even try to offer reissues of older models, but were looking forward to new concepts, like the unconventional three-coil Mother-

*Les Paul Signature with low impedance pickups designed by Bill Lawrence.*

bucker from Mighty Mite, the active models from EMG, and any conceivable replacement parts made from brass, as they were believed to increase sustain.
However, the demand for old style tones was still present, so along came Seymour Duncan, with his SH-1 '59 Model, with plain enamel wire in the coils and, for the first few years, butyrate bobbins and rough cast AlNiCo 5 magnets. Duncan, as a young musician, played in several bands and met a number of famous players such as Robbie Robertson, Jimmy Page, Roy Buchanan and Jimi Hendrix. He also had conversations about tone with Les Paul, Leo Fender and Seth Lover and then worked in the Fender Soundhouse in London, servicing Jeff Beck, Peter Frampton, and The Who.

Duncan built a Telecaster with two humbucking pickups for Jeff Beck, among other things, and finally, in 1976, opened his own pickup factory. Soon Duncan pickups became the obvious choice for any player seeking vintage flavored tones. His models were not accurate replicas by today's standards, but we must remember that no one else was offering vintage voiced pickups at the time.

The DiMarzio Super Distortion and P.A.F. were the most popular replacement pickups of the seventies, and not only famous players (such as Al DiMeola, Ace Frehley, Earl Slick, Frank Marino, Neal Schon and Paul Gilbert, et. al.) used them, but several guitar builders, both American and Japanese, started to offer "DiMarzio Powered" models. By the turn of the eighties, players were divided into two factions: DiMarzio, which were geared toward proponents of hard rock or heavy fusion, and Duncan, for those seeking a more traditional, vintage sound. However, perceptions aside, both companies were soon offering a wide range of models for any style of music and Duncan too could list rock blues players like Dickey Betts, Warren Haynes, and Gary Rossington, along with fusion players like Scott Henderson and Mike Stern, as well as hard rock players like Alex Skolnick, Dimebag Darrell and others as customers.

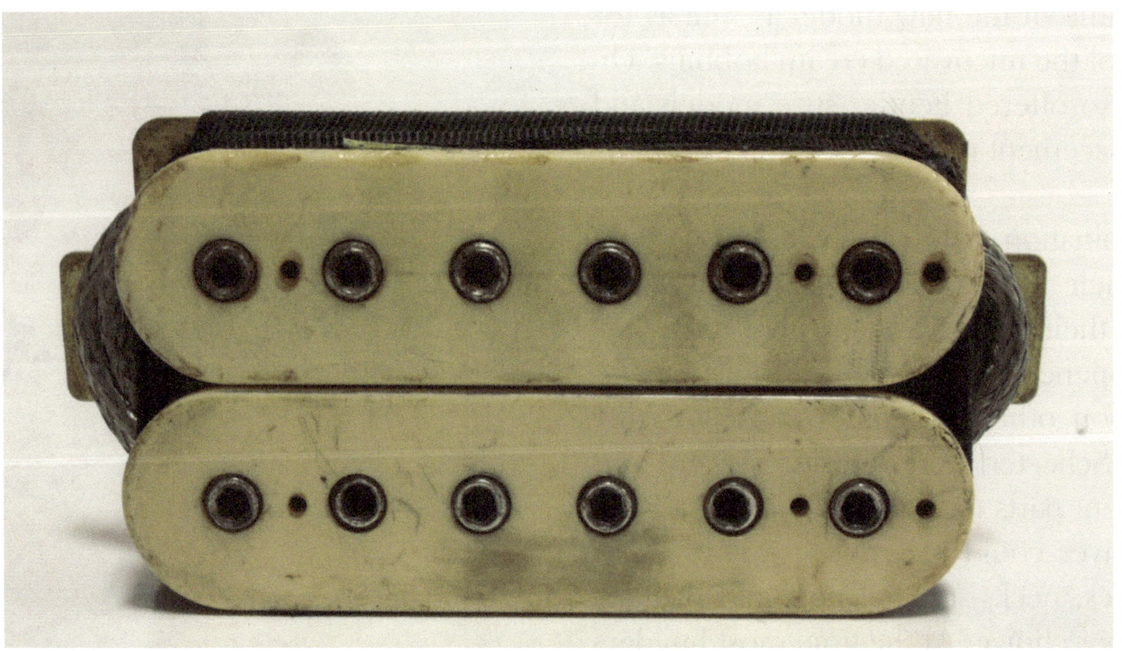

*The DiMarzio Super Distorsion, the most popular replacement pickup of the seventies.*

# Back To The Original Specs

In the eighties, the aftermarket pickups field was dominated by two brands, DiMarzio and Duncan, and both companies made their models available as stock equipment for several guitar builders.

In the meantime, the quest for more power from the pickups started to become less relevant. In the early seventies, amplifier builders were battling distortion as a lack of transparency was deemed a defect. Then Randall Smith introduced the Mesa Boogie amp with an extra gain stage in the preamp to saturate the first stage, which was the beginning of a new kind of amp, the high gain amp. On some models these high gain amps had multiple gain stages, so that players did not have to rely on powerful pickups to get the distortion they wanted as they did with the relatively low gain amps of the past. Many players started to find the old, relatively low output pickups to be preferable for their broader frequency response and greater versatility. The demand for a more accurate reproduction of the traditional models began to grow.

Gibson finally started to respond to the demand for more vintage flavored guitars and issued the Heritage Standard 80 and Heritage Standard 80 Elite Les Pauls which were essentially nothing more than regular Standards with figured maple tops. Regardless, it was a move toward the original look, and Tim Shaw was given the job to research the specs of the old pickups. The resultant model continued to be called "Pat Appl. For", but Shaw was not able to get very far in pursuit of the original specs as so many components (such as the plain enamel wire for the coils and butyrate bobbins) were jettisoned to keep costs down. A compromise, for sure, but the pickups had their own voice

*Gibson Heritage Standard 80 (Left).*
*In 1980 Gibson resumed some of the vintage elements introducing the Heritage Series, with figured tops and Shaw designed pickups.*

*1986 Giibson Les Paul Reissue (Right).*
*In 1985 Gibson tried to get closer to the original vintage specs, a program which would evolve to the creation of the Custom Shop and the Historic Series in 1993 and the True Historic Series in 2015.*

and even today those "Tim Shaw" pickups have their admirers.
In 1990 a new reissue of the original humbucker, was realized, with P.A.F. expert Tom Holmes providing guidance as a consultant. It was called the 57 Classic, and was advertised as the most accurate reissue ever created by the brand. Made with AlNiCo 2 magnet and plain enamel wire for the coils, the new model was a little closer but was still being built with ABS bobbins and was also wax potted. For those seeking a higher output, the 57 Classic Plus offered a slightly over wound version. Unfortunately, to cut costs, Gibson again decided to change the specs and in 2006 they went back to poly coated wire for the coils, which were dyed to resemble plain enamel.

Besides the 59 model, Duncan offered another P.A.F.-inspired model: the SH-PG1 "Pearly Gates". This set was based on the set in the famous 1959 "Pearly Gates" Les Paul owned by Billy Gibbons of ZZ Top. Both sets are wound on an original Leesona 102 winding machine that Duncan bought in the early 1980s in Kalamazoo. It is one of the machines used to wind the original Gibson pickups, but the practice of wax potting and the use of standard materials (to keep the price competitive) prevents them from more closely resembling real P.A.F.s in tone and appearance. However, for those seeking a more vintage accurate and better sounding version, a Custom Shop version of the Pearly Gates is available.

While good enough for most players and popular enough to cement Duncan's dominance in the market, for some connoisseurs and collectors these models were still just not comparable to real P.A.F. pickups. As a result they turned their attention to individual pickup winders such as Tom Holmes (a luthier who originally built guitars for people like Bo Diddley, Billy Gibbons, Albert King and many others, and then began concentrating on winding pickups) and Jim Rolph (who has been building P.A.F. and Fender style pickups since 1978). Both winders were legendary for their great attention to detail and their discriminating use of select materials. Holmes builds the parts he needs for his pickups in his shop from scratch and outsources only the wire and magnets.

In 1992 the Seymour Duncan Custom Shop started offering a new line called the Antiquity Series, with models made to "look, smell and sound" like thirty-year-old, well-used pickups. This humbucking model is, of course, wound on the Leesona winding machine, made with butyrate bobbins, unpotted plain enamel coils, slightly deGaussed AlNiCo 2 magnets ('dun-aged' in Duncan's parlance), and hand-aged covers.

Another Custom Shop offering was the Greenie Model which was inspired by the pickups in the legendary 1959 Les Paul used by Peter Green in the Bluesbreakers and the Fleetwood Mac. This guitar was later sold to Gary Moore and more recently to Kirk Hammett of the heavy metal band Metallica, and features a flipped magnet in the neck unit which gives it a legendary, haunting, out-of-phase sound.

At the time there were no other big companies offering accurate P.A.F. replicas and Duncan proved that there was a market for authentic sounding and looking replicas which opened the door to many new companies specialized in such products. Other small companies appeared on the scene such as Lindy Fralin, Jason Lollar and Wolfetone, which all offered incredible products. The aged look was also quite novel even though guitar restorers and repairmen such as Vince Cunetto and Roger Sadowsky had been aging guitars/parts for years. It was not until 1995 that Fender started offering their "Relic" models. Originally it was J.W. Black's idea while working on a Broadcaster for Ron Wood in 1994, and Keith Richards is also said to have ordered some old looking Telecasters to use while on tour. The idea was a success and later the market was flooded with guitars, pickups and effects artificially aged from the factory to look like their vintage ancestors. Gibson responded with Les Pauls aged by Tom Murphy and proceeded to develop its own proprietary aging process.

In the late 1990s Seymour Duncan offered the SH-55 "Seth Lover" model, designed with the inventor himself as a consultant and meant as a new version of the original Gibson humbucker. The "Seth Lover" had butyrate bobbins, unpotted plain enamel wire and an AlNiCo 2 magnet.

Responding to the market, Gibson introduced the Burstbucker in 2000 and it was available in three output levels. Gibson don't publish the DCR values, as most builders do, but states that the BB-2 is the "normal" wind, the BB-1 is slightly underwound, and the BB-3 is overwound, with a relative output (on a 0-10 scale) of 6.5 for the BB-1, 7.4 for the BB-2, and 8.4 for the BB-3. This model was originally designed to comply with a request from Japanese collectors and differed from the 57 Classic due to its slightly rawer tone and became standard equipment on Gibson Custom Shop Historic line guitars in 2002. Burstbuckers were available unpotted (they were actually lightly potted when installed at the factory and unpotted when sold as an aftermarket item), with plain enamel coils and AlNiCo 2 magnets. The model underwent several changes by the end of the decade and in 2006 the coils were once again made with poly wire, albeit dyed to look like plain enamel (the same production change which affected the 57 Classic).

In 2013, a new model was designed for the Historic line with the help of Ron Ellis: the AlNiCo 3 Custom Bucker, with a clearer and more transparent sound. All the Gibson Reissue models are made with standard materials and remain generic, they aspire to be historically accurate, but lack the use of correct materials and specs that other specialized companies are now offering.
The popularity of vintage Les Pauls and other models from the so called "golden age" of Gibson, continued to grow thanks to players like Slash, Jimmy Page and Gary Moore. Gradually, more small enterprises, such as Van Zandt, Curtis Novak, Don Mare, Peter Florance's Voodoo Pickups, Bare Knuckle Pickups in the UK, Manlius in Germany and many others started offering replacement vintage voiced pickups.

DiMarzio offered several models on the P.A.F. theme, but instead of going the vintage route, preferred to use new designs to get old style tones with his "air" series.

More recent additions to the Duncan Custom Shop P.A.F. offerings are two Limited Edition Joe Bonamassa related models, the Joe Bonamassa Signature and the Skinnerburst Set, based on the P.A.F. pickups on two of the player's original Les Pauls nicknamed Magellan and Principal Skinner.

# P.A.F. Replicas And Clones

The new millennium brought more research and even more accurate reproductions of the original Gibson humbucker. Magnets and metal parts were analyzed to find out the alloys initially used, every detail was scrutinized to determine not only the correct materials, but also the building procedures used on the originals. New companies appeared, committed to reproducing the old models to unprecedented degrees of accuracy in looks and tone.

From the UK came the impressive "Over the Pond Guy" P.A.F. replicas. Available for only a limited time, they were made by a master luthier who preferred to remain anonymous. OTPGs have now achieved mythical status and although they would not be mistaken for genuine P.A.F.s by experts, they are close enough to the vintage P.A.F. look, sound and feel that they remain some of the most sought after P.A.F. replicas on the market. However, finding a set of these might prove difficult since there were very few made they demand a premium, and are extremely difficult to come by.

Other winders such as David Bowes (Sigil Pickups), James Finnerty (ReWind Electric Guitar Pickups), Jon Gundry (Throbak Electronics), Mick McGinnis (Manlius Guitar Pickups), Bill Megela (Electric City Pickups), Tim Mills (Bare Knuckle Pickups), Spencer Mumford (Shed Pickups), David Shepherd (Mojotone Pickups), Jeff (Shep) Shepherd (Sheptone Pickups), Dave Stephens (Stephens Design Pickups), Mark Stow (Ox4 Pickups), and Aleksandar Vrhovec (Wizz Pickups), established themselves for accuracy, and they're just a few of the new winders all around the world offering the widest range of choices ever seen. Duane Flowers, who has compiled a very comprehensive list of pickup winders, took the time to find out how many builders there are on the market and discovered over 350 brands, with more being reported every day!

Specifically, what is it that makes a humbucking pickup a proper P.A.F. replica?

We would call a pickup a replica if it is made using the correct components and building procedures, for example, using low carbon alloys for the metallic parts, nickel silver without a copper layer for the covers, butyrate bobbins, magnets charged to vintage specs, plain enamel wire and machine wound coils. They should also be unpotted and wound to the proper capacitance and DC resistance.

In reality, many pickup builders do not conform to our strict definition and would argue that accurate sonic results can be obtained using different procedures and materials and the term "replica", in the marketplace, is used with a much broader interpretation.

Even if today commercial components made from "vintage" alloys are available, the best winders prefer to have them custom made or to build most of the parts in their own shops using raw materials of their own choosing to maintain the greatest control over quality and accuracy. Wire and magnets are also often ordered to spec. Having everything custom-made makes the products more expensive, but these builders claim it is the only way to guarantee absolute authenticity regarding tone and aesthetics.

Nowadays, many sets are also aged to match the look of the originals. This aging process adds to the total cost as the process is time-consuming to the point that the covers alone may be as expensive as a set of cheap off-the-shelf pickups. However, this is ultimately important to the sound because covers always cause a slight decrease in the pickup's response to higher frequencies. Cheap covers may be too thick and usually, to make the plating easier, have a layer of copper under the nickel plating further sacrificing tone and adding to the loss in transparency.

There is also quite a bit of debate between the virtues of machine winding versus that of hand winding (or hand-guided winding). For a long time hand winding was perceived as a true craftsman's approach as opposed to commercial machine winding, in the sense that it offered greater accuracy than what the big companies could offer and was truer to the way vintage pickups were built. Of course, if the winder knows his stuff, both methods can guarantee good sounding pickups, but, all being equal, there is a difference. First, Gibson pickups were always machine wound, and Seth Lover attested to that in many interviews concerning them. Some experts in the field, like Dave Stephens, believe that since the beginning, starting with the "Charlie Christian" Bar Pickup, all Gibson pickups were machine wound. So to be historically correct, that is the only way to make a P. A. F. Replica (or, for that matter, a replica of any other Gibson model). Fender pickups, on the other hand, at least until CBS took over, had always been made by hand guiding the wire.

The idea that old pickups were hand wound comes from the fact that they seemed to be scatter wound with some random pattern in the coils, as opposed to the very regular pattern of modern machine wound coils. However, there is a difference. The irregularities in the machine's patterns were programmed to repeat in a more predictable manner, while any irregularities due to hand winding were unintentional. So the tone of a Gibson pickup was less clinical, with a richer harmonic content, than modern pickups, but with a less casual scatter than a typical Fender pickup, and thus retained a distinct edge in the highest frequencies. They could both be called scatter wound, but the way the scatter occurred was different.

Some winders, who want to be historically and sonically accurate, use different methods and machines depending on what kind of pickup they aim to replicate, some, however, think that with experience and a trained hand, the differences are negligible.

Tom Holmes, for example, used both methods at first in accordance with his customer's wishes. After a while, when customers believed that anything "hand made" was superior to anything "machine made", he became so accustomed to using the hand guided method that he now prefers to continue in the same way, even if he thinks that it may result in slight variations in tone.

One thing that is not historically accurate is the configuration of most sets, usually with dedicated neck and bridge pickups. This predetermination is something that Gibson never did. Gibson did

*Assorted Gibson Reissues, Signatures Models and Collector's Choice Models each with aftermarket P.A.F. pickups selected for their unique sonic qualities.*

*2011 Gibson Historic Les Paul R8.*

*2009 Gibson VOS Billy Gibbons "Pearly Gates" Signature and 2013 Gibson Collector's Choice #8 1959 Les Paul aka "The Beast" with aftermarket P.A.F. replica pickups.*

not offer sets with different specs for each position until the early seventies, when they introduced SG models with ceramic Super Humbucking pickups.

Since then almost all manufacturers offer "calibrated" sets which are compensated in output and tone for their intended positions. The reason for this being that at the bridge the vibration of the strings is weaker than that near the fingerboard. So the solution was to have more turns of wire, which results in more power and stronger mids on the bridge unit and fewer turns, hence a clearer tone, at the neck position.

While many could perceive this as an improvement, the randomly fitted pickups of the original guitars are part of the charm of those instruments. Having both pickups almost the same, or installed randomly regardless of the specs, requires more work on the part of the musician, who must compensate by more extensively using the volume and tone controls to balance his tones. This workload is evidenced by watching videos of players like Jimmy Page, Peter Green and other classic rock heroes in which it is easy to see how they were always fiddling with their guitar's knobs. The reward of this randomness is a broader range of sounds, from thick, vocal neck tones to cutting, bright bridge tones and a fuller mid position with many more nuances available through the judicious use of the guitar's controls. It was common at the time to try to get a broad range of tones and, to that end, it seems that Fender even used to purposely install the higher reading unit in the neck slot of the Stratocasters.

Some winders now offer sets inspired by specific guitars and if those instruments had a higher reading pickup in the neck, so too will the replica set.

ReWind Electric has a line of pickups called "True Kalamazoo" that are made even to be "philosophically" accurate. These are designed with sets made to replicate not only the specs of the originals but also some "time correct" randomness in matching the coils and the units for each set. The choice of magnets, the color of the bobbins and the winding patterns are all accurate for the chosen year, so, for example, there are no zebra or white bobbins on a 1958 set. This randomness is just how it would have been if a customer were ordering a set from Gibson in the fifties or early sixties.

In regard to P.A.F. Replicas we are referring to pickups made with the same procedures, materials and specs of the originals, but not intending to copy any specific set. When speaking of P.A.F. "Clones" we are referring to exact copies of a specific original set.

Just to give some examples, Wizz Pickups calls his standard model "P.A.F. Premium Clones" because it is faithful in every detail to a vintage set he loved and used as a blueprint for this model. Throbak offers the MT-102B set, based on the pickups of the Les Paul used by Keith Richards and Mick Taylor in the early seventies. ReWind Electric offers the P.A.F.-1 Set, which is a copy of an original '59 set.

Sometimes cloning a set is not so easy. Electric City offers a Limited Edition "Hallowed Ground" Set, cloned after the P.A.F.s of a very fine sounding original 1958 Les Paul. The original set used wire that was out of spec and the availability of that particular wire is quite scarce, so it is only possible to make a limited number of sets and resume production when and if more wire with the necessary specs is located.

When asked about the possibility of getting enough data to clone a set via nondestructive methods, Jon Gundry answered:

*Yes and no. Without taking apart the pickup there is a limit to what can be known. However I can extrapolate quite a bit based upon the era of the P.A.F., Gauss readings at the poles and resistance at a known temperature and inductance readings and comparing them against data accumulated over the years. You can even determine if the magnet is short or long without taking the cover off by using magnetic viewing film. Even then you need to do some magnet swapping to hear which magnet is the closest match at the given Gauss. At the very least you can get enough data for a good starting point to replicate a given set.*

As with the term "replica", the term "clone" is often used with a broader interpretation than intended. Some sets are "more" than exact copies of original sets in the sense that they are more "closely inspired by" the reference set, and then tweaked to make them more balanced for the modern player.

During the last ten years the research carried on by the best winders and their willingness to share their results has not only expanded our knowledge on what many call the "holy grail" of vintage tones, but has also made it possible to reproduce that tone with unprecedented accuracy. To some vintage enthusiasts there is still nothing that can compare to the original P.A.F., and its historical importance is not debatable, but the truth is that today's replicas are very, very close and the research continues.

Many details have been uncovered concerning metal alloys, magnets, wire specs, etc., but all the originals were different, from one to the next, to some extent, and of course to prefer one sample out of several is a matter of personal preference. So, while each winder offers models patterned after different units, each builder makes his choices according to his preferences in tone. Mark Stow of Ox4 Pickups told us:

*To my ears, a good P.A.F. will have a snappy clear tone, at any volume. The ones I played have had a lovely top end bite and respond very well when rolling down the volume on the guitar. In my experience the sparkle tone of the P.A.F. is down to the windings of the bobbins. Listen to Mike Bloomfield's "Mary Ann" THAT IS THE TONE! The dynamics of his attack on the strings and volume knob is coming through those P.A.F.s. It's bright but warm with a top end bite. Perfect example of a great sounding P.A.F.*

Of course a winder will not just copy any old P.A.F. that he comes across, he will only put effort into those he deems worthy, and of course, that choice is always subjective. He would also probably continue to further tweak his model in accordance with his own personal tastes in tone. Some may like their P.A.F.s veering on the warm side of the spectrum while others prefer brighter examples, thus, with so many variables present in the originals there is quite a bit of room for interpretation. Consequently, every brand has its own sonic fingerprint regardless of the specific model being copied. Of course famous players and recordings are often used as a reference for the potential buyer and all winders are aware that a pickup can sound very different in reality than how it sounds in a recorded session, where the amp, effects and sound engineer's work (not to mention the player's technique) definitively change how the tone will be perceived in the end.

So, why there are so many different replicas on the market? Simply because there are so many different originals to choose from, and each builder will focus on different aspects/characteristics when designing his interpretation. Even if one winder offers ten different models representing a broad range of variance, using different magnets or coil combinations, there is still room for competitors to put other nuances on the table.

Of course, with so many builders in the field, while many are committed to their craft and passionate about recreating the originals as accurately as possible, others only claim to make P.A.F. replicas to sell average humbucking models. Not everybody has the talent, the will, and the knowledge necessary to make authentic sounding P.A.F.s and there will always be those asserting that even the best ones do not match the originals 100%. The best winders work hard to build up a reputation and happy customers are their best advertisement.

The choice is not easy, and we must always remember that all pickups sound different on different guitars and through different amps when played with different fingers, and the lust for the ideal tone can be addictive and expensive even if we rely on the best builders. The problem is that there is no convincing method to translate the specs in a handy set of data that helps the customer chose between different brands/models without trying a set on his or her guitar. So only the description from the manufacturer can offer some clue as to their actual performance. The only universally reported spec is the DC resistance, but we know now how deceiving that can be. Possibly, the next step would not be as concerned with building more accurate pickups, which is always possible, but rather in finding a way to communicate a shared set of metrics that would give the customer the information necessary to make a better, more informed decision, even if the subjective nature of guitar pickups makes it quite difficult even to imagine how to achieve such an aim. In the meantime, the best thing we can do is to get in touch with the winder of choice and be very clear about our preferences. Most of the time their experience will be such that they can guide us through the different models and specs to get as close as possible to our dream sound.

# Appendixes

## P.A.F. Q&A

## Interviews to the Winders

## David Bowes

## Jon Gundry

## Jason Lollar

## Wolfe Mcleod

## Tim Mills

## Dave Stephens

## Aleksandar Vrhovec

# P.A.F. Q&A

**I've seen a P.A.F. with tape around the bobbins that is dark green instead of the usual black, is it original?**

In my experience, nearly all, if not entirely all, of the black paper tape on P.A.F.s and patent decal pickups all the way through the 1960s had a dark greenish hue in the right light. How much of that green hue appears seems to be a factor of both lighting and the life of the pickup. The more dried out the tape is, the more the green seems to become prominent. The green may be a result of some component of the adhesive, which eventually evaporates through the paper portion of the tape staining it. The green may also be an ingredient in the black color of the paper portion of the tape and, as the tape ages and dries out, the green becomes more obvious. (James Finnerty)

**Since on the original pickups the wire used in the coils used to vary so much in specs, is it even possible today to rewind a pickup or replicate it with the same tone?**

Possibly, yes, but only with a great deal of luck or a great deal of effort! In the coil wire used on P.A.F.s, not only did the wire core thickness vary but the insulation thickness also varied independently, and both to a greater degree than today's wire tolerance specifications allow. Also, not only did these properties of the wire vary from one spool to the next, but through the entire length of a single spool. So, with a great deal of luck a winder may find a vintage P.A.F. with an exceptionally rare regularity to the copper core and insulation thickness of the coil wire along its length. With an even greater deal of luck that same P.A.F. may have an exceptionally rare regularity to the copper core and insulation thicknesses of the coil wire on both coils. Then, with a still greater amount of luck, one may be able to find two spools of modern wire that have similar properties to the vintage example being reproduced and be able to make a reasonable replication of it. This is similar to how vintage P.A.F. and other pickup repairs are done at ReWind and having a large selection of new wire, and a nice stash of old wire, helps with that. For a replication of coils for a production model pickup, there is another option. When you have a specific pickup which has a voice that meets certain goals or is novel or otherwise exceptional in some desirable way, and you want to make many coils inspired by its own, then one can consider if a custom run of plain enamel wire from one of the factories is cost-beneficial. With several ReWind Electric production model humbuckers the wire core thickness, wire insulation thickness, and average variance along the length of the original coil from start to finish has been measured and then reproduced in the wire manufacturing process to create spools which, when combined with the corresponding coil patterns and shape and the rest of the pickup, give truly accurate results of individual coils which were found to be exceptional examples of vintage voiced pickups. So creating extremely accurate replicas can be done with the right budget, equipment and knowledge. (James Finnerty)

**I've seen many players using their P.A.F.s without covers, why do they take them off?**

On original P.A.F.s, early players most likely took the covers off for aesthetics or as a result of performing repairs requiring cover removal. Though an original P.A.F. cover can slightly adjust an upper resonant peak and drop-off of treble response, the pickup's adjustable height and pole screws make a far more significant difference. A few well-known individuals playing uncovered P.A.F.s likely started a style trend. Later on, gaining momentum in the 1970s, an aftermarket parts industry began to grow and many players and builders used brass parts which were popular at the time, including covers. Brass covers will much more significantly reduce the treble and alter the upper-frequency response of a guitar pickup more than the nickel silver material that original P.A.F. covers were made from. This is likely the time and reason for the (not untrue) belief that, at least many and especially cheaper, pickup covers will reduce treble and change the voice of a pickup. Early Telecaster neck pickups used brass covers, with the darker sound likely being the very intent, as Leo had taken several steps to make the neck pickup on these guitars the "bass" pickup. It should be noted that P.A.F.s and early T-Tops were never intended for use without a cover. They are fragile and many frail parts are not well protected without a cover. Playing uncovered vintage humbuckers will near certainly shorten their life but by how much is case-by-case per the player and environment. Wax potting a vintage pickup does not properly address the exposed fragile parts and is detrimental to the voice of the pickup and its value so should not be considered an alternative to a cover. In the late 1970s Gibson first introduced some factory uncovered humbuckers. They were T-Tops and used some different parts including PVC coil tape, bobbins without coil windows, plastic spacers, and poly insulated coil wire, all of which may help improve longevity without a protective metal cover. (James Finnerty)

**What key factors should I be aware of when buying an original P.A.F. online?**

A fraudulent P.A.F. market exists and is persistent. Makers of fake P.A.F.s and fake parts are regularly addressing their shortcomings which previously gave many fake P.A.F.s away as being fraudulent. To date, however, the counterfeiters have always been a few steps behind and just can't manage to get everything right. In the day of technology being hacked and leaked before something is even officially released, I find it impressive that those wishing to reproduce a 60+-year-old product in form and function have fallen so short over such a long period of attempts. It is both a testimony to the quality and uniqueness of Kalamazoo-Gibson's product and an example of how a low budget attempt to replicate a product made with pride and quality old world manufacturing will only fool those who are not familiar with the original article. Many visual aspects can give away a fake P.A.F. The most obvious, and probably the most ignored, is the price. If a deal is too good to be true – especially with a product so famous the world over, that should be a sign to the buyer that something is not as stated. Nearly everyone who asks me to look at an eBay auction, seeking my opinion on a supposed P.A.F. for sale, sends me a link to someone selling a modern fake for only a few hundred dollars. In today's market, an uncovered, double black, well-used, gold-hardware P.A.F. (generally the least expensive P.A.F.) is still valued at or near $2,000 USD. If you think you found the deal of a lifetime and are getting a real P.A.F. for only a few hundred dollars from someone who does not know what they have and are doing, reconsider the odds of you getting this once in a lifetime deal versus getting the all too common modern fake. Many of the fake P.A.F.s I see are just modern Gibson '57 Classics, poorly aged and in blurry photos, hoping to catch an overly hopeful buyer before they have time to consider and look into it properly. Some visual signs to look into when shopping for a P.A.F. can be helpful, also. The ideal situation is a P.A.F. with its cover still originally soldered on and the lead still originally soldered into a vintage Gibson guitar. That is not as common though, unless you are taking the whole guitar home, which could be a great idea but isn't always possible. Original cover solder is a sign that the P.A.F. has not been tampered with too much. An expert can make a repaired pickup look to be originally soldered, however, so this alone is not a deal-maker. Parts of a P.A.F. copy that forgers generally get wrong are the shape and material of the cover, the plating method of the cover, the style of the braided shield hookup wiring, the Patent Applied For decals, the shape of the feet on the baseplate, the "L" marks on the feet of the baseplate, the style of pole piece holes in the baseplate, the location and size of the hole where the braided shield enters the baseplate, the shape, slot size, and plating method of the pole screws, the chamfer, the plating method of the cover, the cutoff tooling marks of the slugs, the shape and size of the four brass screw heads and the threading of the brass screws. Usually, it is a combination of several things that don't add up which gives away a fake. More recently, we are seeing more partially vintage and partially modern pickups posing as P.A.F.s in an attempt to relieve an uneducated buyer of their money. The best practice would be to have the pickup professionally authenticated and to buy from a reputable source. (James Finnerty)

### My P.A.F. sounds lifeless and weak, should I replace the magnet?

There are a number of reasons a once-working P.A.F. can now sound weaker than it used to, including partial shorts, a single coil operating, an open coil that is capacitive coupling and still partially working, and problems with the magnet. At ReWind many vintage magnets have been observed to be only partially charged or charged off-axis or in a non-uniform method. Sometimes, the magnet is just made in such a way that it does not hold an even charge across its length, but sometimes a perfectly fine magnet was either not charged straight or fully across its length, or its field has become weakened or misaligned over time by external electromagnetic forces. The proper way to address this is to measure and note the magnet's Gauss at several points across both of its polar surfaces, fully charge the magnet with a suitable electrical charging unit, let the magnet settle for some time, and measure and note the Gauss again. If the Gauss is reading consistently higher and even across the polar surfaces, the magnet should be at least as good as new now. If there is a significantly uneven set of readings along the polar surfaces, the magnet may be flawed in nature and replacement may be a better option. Generally, P.A.F.s and all vintage Gibson magnets tend to respond very well to a full and even charging. Occasionally, there will be one with a problem, however. Vintage Fender rod magnets can have this problem as well. Sometimes due to voids in the magnetic alloy during casting. (James Finnerty)

**I bought a set of P.A.F. replicas but when I compared them to the original pickups on a friend's vintage guitar they sounded different. What's up with that?**

P.A.F.s were not consistent in sound or design from one to the next, particularly the earlier ones. For a modern replica to sound like a vintage P.A.F., it has to be a replica (and a good one at that) of that particular P.A.F., or at least one very similar in composition and design to it. Towards the end of P.A.F. production in the 1960s, P.A.F.s had become far more consistent, so, while there may not be a specific "early P.A.F. sound" there is something of a "late P.A.F. sound" where there were fewer variables to consider. Though there were still some all the way to the end, including magnets, which can be a significant factor in the resulting voice of a P.A.F. (James Finnerty)

**If the original pickups were meant to be the same for neck and bridge, why do I always see replicas labeled according to the specified position?**

The originals were installed randomly, regardless of the respective DCR values, so sometimes the highest reading one came to the neck position, but since the seventies most companies started to offer models designed specifically for the neck and bridge positions and it was thought to be an improvement. People got so used to having a different type for each position that now that is what they want even with replicas. Some companies are now offering sets with pickups that can be used either way or replicas of original sets which had the "hotter" unit in the neck. We encourage players to try both positions, if the difference in reading is not too extreme, to swap pickups regardless of the labeling, as both configurations can offer distinctive tones with a broader overall range and a fuller middle position when the hotter one is in the neck slot. Which way is better depends on the specific set, the player's taste, style and, of course, the guitar. For some reason it seems that a hotter neck model works best if on the guitar is used vintage correct hardware (light aluminum tailpiece with steel studs, brass bridge posts), as the modern hardware seems to emphasize the fundamentals and more easily make the sound potentially muddy in that position. (Mario Milan)

Some original P.A.F.s had a narrow spacing for the neck pickup, but this is rare and nearly all vintage P.A.F.s are spaced the same and intended for use in any position on a guitar - neck, middle or bridge. Some Varitone equipped guitars have shown to have reverse magnetic polarity in one pickup, which may have been intentional, making another case for a "neck pickup" versus a "bridge pickup". However, this is also rare and is not even the case in all Varitone equipped Gibsons, which could make it nothing more than coincidence, accident, or experimentation. For the most part, at Kalamazoo Gibson, a humbucker was a humbucker. As players, techs, builders and engineers all moved forward in their craft it became a growing trend to put a pickup with more output in the bridge position, where the strings move less over it, and to put a pickup with lower output in the neck position, where the strings move a great deal more over it. This helped balance out the volume of the two pickups. If one were to put the exact same pickup in each position, it would be found to have much more volume and bass in the neck position. This is simply because the pickup is located closer to the center of the guitar and the center of the strings, meaning the strings vibrate in a wider arc at this point. The bridge pickup is near the end of the strings where they hardly move at all, so more output in this position will give a more powerful electrical output to the neck pickup at the output jack of the guitar. This phenomenon can be observed with a typical acoustic guitar. Strumming the strings near the last fret at the neck joint will give a full and loud sound while strumming the strings right up against the bridge will result in a very thin and quieter sound. (James Finnerty)

### If a P.A.F. does not produce any sound and gives no reading should I have it rewound?

Getting no resistance reading on a meter means there is an open circuit, either from a break in the coil or a break somewhere else in the wiring. Getting a full short means there is likely a problem in the wiring of the pickup, but could still indicate some type of problem with the coils. Corrosion from moisture, the elements, sweat, and the natural electrical reactions that take place where two types of metals meet in guitar pickups are the most common reasons for failures. Tampering is next. If a P.A.F. does not sound or read on a meter as expected, it is best not to touch it and contact an experienced professional who will be able to guide you through some questions and instruct you to the proper course of action. (James Finnerty)

### How should I adjust a P.A.F. pickup for the best tone?

One way is to keep the adjustable screws almost level with the cover and raise the whole pickup as close as possible to the strings while pressing on the last fret, then lower it by the two adjustable screws on the sides, little by little until the desired balance between power and clarity is reached. The closer to the strings, the fuller the sound will be, the further from the strings, the more the tone will be clean and clear. Even a quarter turn can make a big difference, so proceed slowly, listening for any difference. If the distance is too great the tone can become lifeless and too weak, so it is important to find the sweet spot. There is no set rule, as differences in magnet's strength, number of turns in the coils, the kind of strings used and preferences in tone quality call for slightly different adjustments in each case. It also depends on the guitar's resonant qualities and amp's characteristics. For the best results it is important to be patient and spend some time trying different heights. Then, when a pretty good balance is achieved, it is possible to fine tune the sound by adjusting the pole pieces string to string, again turning the screws a little while continually checking the overall tone. It is important to note that raising or lowering the poles changes the shape of the magnetic field and affects the tone of the whole pickup, not just the individual strings. (Mario Milan)

Fret or capo all strings at the last fret. Raise the pickups up to where the pole pieces are just about touching the strings, evenly on both sides. Put a driver's license, business card, or similar between the pickup and strings. It should be held there by the string pressure.

While holding the guitar in the playing position, lower the pickup evenly by half turns of the height adjustment screws until the license falls free. That is the closest to the strings that you are going to want your pickups, otherwise they may hit the strings when you play hard. From this point, I would plug into a loud, and just a little overdriven, amp with plenty of headroom and start playing and lowering the pickups until they are in the sweet spot that results in the voicing you prefer. That will be different on every guitar and may be different across the strings/neck so you have a bit of compromise to make.

Always start with the neck pickup. It is much easier to get a good tone out of, and dial in, a bridge pickup to match the neck pickup than the other way around, so start with the neck. What you are really looking for is two things - that the magnetism of the pickup does not pull the strings too much and produces unwanted artificial harmonics (this mainly happens on neck pickups with stronger magnets), and that the long tail of the sustaining note evolves in a pleasing way as it decays. You will hear that note tail change in complex ways as it gets very quiet near the end of its sustain. That is why you want a loud amp, with a touch of gain, to enhance the ability to hear that. You can now try raising or lowering the pickup evenly on both sides by a half or full turn of the screws at a time to see what the overall tonal difference is. Pickups can be very sensitive and responsive to this. See what you like. You can make a pickup brighter/warmer and more or less dynamic by adjusting its height.

Once you get the overall height how you like it, you can adjust the height adjustment screws independently to angle the pickup in the ring. I tend to lower the bass side a bit to help enhance the unwound strings on most P.A.F.-types, but it is entirely a matter of preference and each guitar/pickup combination will respond a little differently.

Now that you've got the neck pickup dialed in, repeat the same procedure with the bridge. Once you have that set, play a little bit while flipping the 3-way switch through all three positions. Adjust the bridge pickup, trying to get the balance of volume that you prefer in the neck and bridge positions (not everyone wants both pickups even) and also try to get a middle position sound that you truly like. I do this part by adjusting the bridge pickup only and leaving the neck where I liked it best. I like to set them up for a great chirpy nasal honk on the note attack in the middle position. Some prefer more neck or bridge dominance when in the middle.

After this, you will probably want to adjust your amp settings again, to match your new guitar/pickup sound. Adjust the amp while on the neck pickup. Always work on the neck pickup, and then match the bridge to that. That is my theory. Step away from the room for a while to "re-calibrate" your ears to the world and then come back and repeat the fine tuning. Maybe even give it a few days or try in another room or rig. The mind can play tricks on you and "compensates" when you listen to the same thing for too long so it is good to step away sometimes.

A note on adjustable pole pieces - use these to balance the sound of the individual coils in a humbucker or to favor specific strings. Raising the pole screws and lowering the entire pickup by the same amount will give you more of the sound of the screw coil. Doing the opposite will give you more the sound of the slug coil. This is preference here and also a matter of matching the pickups to the guitar. In your particular pickup set, you will likely find that you get a brighter sound by balancing the pole screws and height screws to favor the screw coils. You might get more chirp/honk sound with the two coils closely balanced, and a warmer overall sound when you favor the slug coils. After setting the overall height of the pole screws, adjust for individual string balance. (James Finnerty)

### What will happen if I replace the pole pieces in a P.A.F. or replica pickup?

Shorter or longer threaded pole pieces, larger or smaller screw heads, and rounder or pointier shapes can all alter the sound, as well as alloy material and overall mass. Shorter screws result in brighter sounds and longer screws result in a little less treble. Gibson used various length pole screws in other pickups but the length of almost all P.A.F.s through T-Top screws is the same. Gibson did use at least two distinctly different alloys and shape poles in this period which result in different sounds. (James Finnerty)

### P.A.F. pickups and replicas are not potted, how can I avoid feedback issues?

The important thing is that every component of the pickup is firmly assembled with tight tolerance parts. Contrary to popular belief, the problems are mostly caused by poor fit than the coils, unless those are wound too loosely. Such tight tolerance is difficult to achieve on a high production schedule, that is why commercial pickups are potted, the cheapest ones quite heavily. Then, of course, it is important to pay attention to the player's position toward the amplifier, using feedback musically is an art in itself. What a musician does not want is uncontrolled feedback and that should be possible to avoid with good pickups. Another source of vibration can be the cover, so putting a little piece of foam or tape between the top of the bobbins and the cover before soldering it can help to prevent feedback. In some cases even putting tape also on the sides of the pickup. If the music style calls for a large amount of high gain at very high sound levels, maybe a P.A.F. pickup or replica is not the right model. (Mario Milan)

P.A.F. pole screws are notoriously loose. I see this across all P.A.F.s through T-Tops. The slugs are also loose in some and I see this more towards the end of P.A.F.s and the beginning of the pre-T-Tops and continuing. Pole screws that rattle around, vibrating sympathetically with the music, can cause squealing feedback. Slugs doing the same can also cause feedback. Loose pole screws can also mean loose keeper bars and using rough cast magnets results in a loose tolerance for how tightly held the magnet is against the underside of the bobbins, the baseplate, the keeper bar and the slugs. Generally, there is a gap somewhere but each magnet is unique due to its casting. Covers can vibrate against the top parts of the pickups and loose wiring can vibrate inside the covers. The height adjustment springs and the braided shield wiring can even vibrate and be a hard to find the cause of excessive feedback. I always look for something mechanically loose first and firm it up using materials and methods that are not permanent with vintage gear. Potting should not even be a last resort; it is the wrong solution for a vintage pickup every time. Many companies make vintage voice inspired pickups that are mechanically more stable than vintage pickups and can hold up against higher gain and sound pressure levels. (James Finnerty)

## What are lightly potted pickups?

Any time the coils are potted, tone suffers, it does not matter if heavily or lightly, as potting, as light as can be, makes the coils rigid. Some builders apply the potting only to the underside of the pickup to keep the metallic parts from vibrating, and this can help somewhat. (Mario Milan)

"Lightly potted" is actually nothing more than a trend of a catchphrase. Just a made up term popular at the moment which describes dunking the coils or entire pickup into a bath of hot wax. This by definition is "potting" a pickup. "Lightly" doesn't mean anything sonically beneficial, since a single molecule thick layer of wax is all that is needed on a length of coil wire to effectively wax pot it, significantly eliminating its ability to resonate acoustically. Any amount of wax at all in a coil will essentially glue each turn of a coil to its neighboring turns and simultaneously add mass to the coil. This prevents the hair-thin coil wire turns from acoustically vibrating, resulting in feedback with high gain and high SPL conditions. This very same function of even a molecule-thick wax layer preventing the coil turns from vibrating also deadens a pickup's acoustic response to the acoustic vibrations of the instrument, which is one of the most desirable qualities of a beautiful sounding vintage guitar pickup. Since the phenomena responsible for both coil squeal feedback and an open, breathy, acoustically responsive pickup is the same – vibrations of the coil wire turns, one can either stop both or stop none via wax potting. Therefore, if a wax potting is effective at all against coil squeal feedback (and it will be at even the lightest or thinnest possible amount) then it must also be effective at eliminating the more subtle acoustic responsiveness of a great coil because both are the result of the same vibrating coil effect. (James Finnerty)

## Why are replacement covers so expensive?

Labor. Modern inexpensive basic covers are drawn (which is the way the material is formed on a die) and cut in a single step. Original covers were deep-drawn to depth in multiple steps, and then cut flush in another. Modern inexpensive basic covers are copper plated, then buffed, then nickel plated. Original covers were ground and polished to a perfect smooth finish instead of copper plated. Copper plating is faster and cheaper and fills in the little holes and imperfections to get a much faster smooth surface, ready for nickel. Unfortunately, copper alters the sound of pickups and makes them look ugly as they age. Skipping the grinding and polishing step of original covers also results in modern covers having more rounded over corners, while the original P.A.F.s had a flatter TV screen style front shape to them. This flatter front face, and its particular shaped edges, is a result of the hand grinding of the raw nickel silver material cover after drawing and cutting but before nickel plating. There is also a great deal of effort that goes into designing and manufacturing an authentic looking cover which is made on modern tools at a modern factory. One has to account for, in design, the shape that will eventually result after hand processing is done that modifies the shape in the middle. In that regard, one cannot simply laser scan a vintage set of P.A.F. covers and have the tooling made from them, because those vintage covers were modified in shape by hand after machining. One has to calculate and account for those shape differences. Getting the dimpling of the covers right and the cutoff on the bottom is another problem that I faced with ReWind's replica covers. The dimpling around the pole screw holes is a result of both the type of tooling used and again, the hand grinding and buffing. So the tooling has to be right and the technicians also have to be trained on how to create a result through their work that would typically be considered an undesirable feature by today's standards. It all adds up to manual labor costs more than a chemical parts bath and the few people that care for the finest details must pay the price. (James Finnerty)

**I see on the market all the magnet grades supposedly used in original P.A.F. pickups, so why are some replica builders using custom made magnets?**

There are a number of reasons to go with custom magnets as a builder. Custom cast AlNiCo magnets can provide consistency over time. The physical shape and size of magnets contribute to their voice in a guitar pickup so altering these properties can tune the sonic response of a magnet. Custom material blends and manufacturing processes can result in magnets with altered magnetic and sonic properties.

When I was first experimenting with AlNiCo magnets it became obvious quickly that fully charged magnets of a given grade from various sources sounded quite noticeably different when swapping them in the same pickup. Even magnets of a given grade from the same foundry or distributor will vary in a way that significantly changes the voice of a pickup from one lot to the next. Now, with better gear and processes, I can quantify those differences in sonic and magnetic measurements. Having magnets custom made in quantity contributes to consistent sounding pickups over the period of production because a company will have a large stock of the same run of magnets on hand for years' worth of pickup building.

Changing the size and shape of a given grade of a cast AlNiCo magnet will alter its sonic properties. This is particularly the case when changing the polar face surface dimensions. A long list of dimensional and magnetic measurements of Gibson AlNiCo magnets, from the beginning of the 1940s to the late 1970s when Gibson started introducing ceramic magnets into their pickups, shows that Gibson has used many sizes and AlNiCo grades of magnets. Even just within the P.A.F.-era from 1957 through the mid-1960s the dimensions and grade varied with some pattern (and many exceptions). Going earlier to P 90s and their predecessor pickups, the variance becomes even greater with double-thick A3s and single-side-only ground A2 and A3 magnets appearing in a large number of early 50s Gibson pickups (these continue to show up later, occasionally well into the humbucker era). One thing that is very interesting to note is that changing the dimensions in the same way can have very different sonic results in different AlNiCo alloys. For instance, reducing a typical 2.5" long A5 magnet down to 2.25" will result in less treble and more midrange and an overall warmer sounding pickup. Making the same reduction in the polar face length of a 2.5" A2 magnet, however, will have nearly the opposite sonic result, a reduction in bass and mids, becoming an overall brighter sounding pickup.

Altering the blends of the elements used to make AlNiCo magnets can result in sonic changes. AlNiCo magnet alloys were generally engineered to provide the strongest cohesive magnetic force at the time, with each AlNiCo grade becoming stronger. Cohesive force is just one of many properties an AlNiCo magnet exhibits in a guitar pickup and is not nearly the most important. Manipulating the elemental content of an AlNiCo alloy away from the stated standard for that alloy can result in interesting sonic changes in the way a magnet responds... or it might not. There is no charted formula for this. Some of the elements should not be adjusted because they are necessary for the magnet to properly solidify or remain the proper hardness when cooled. It is all an experiment, in this area. I am graphing changes as I go through this very process myself. It is a slow and expensive process, especially when a company does not own a magnet foundry/plant.

Similarly to altering the blend of elements in the alloy, the processes for manufacturing can also be altered away from the stated standard for changes in sonic response. As an example many may be familiar with, there is a now common magnet type commonly referred to as "unoriented" or "isotropic" A5. This unoriented magnet leaves out a step that would normally take place during the manufacturing of an A5 alloy. After the raw AlNiCo material is cast into green sand molds, the molds are broken apart and the still hot AlNiCo bars are then treated with a series of heating and cooling periods, sometimes within a strong magnetic field which allows the internal structure of the magnet to retain an aligned orientation after cooling. This is what makes the magnet the "oriented" type and not the unoriented type. The industrial reason behind this is that oriented AlNiCo blends can exhibit a stronger maximum cohesive force for the same alloy blend, shape, and size of the magnet. The reason pickup builders care about this in A5 magnets is that an unoriented A5 will give a pickup a less harsh treble and a smoother midrange than an oriented or "anisotropic" magnet of the same alloy. Adjusting the heating and cooling time and temperature schedule can also result in altered sonic properties. This, similarly to adjusting the elemental content, is an experimental area right now. It does seem that adjusting these properties can alter the frequency response, of at least some AlNiCo blends, in a pickup. (James Finnerty)

# Interviews with the Winders

The Gibson "Patent Applied For" pickup has been considered a reference point for many pickup builders, and many pickup manufacturers still use this model as the main inspiration for their own interpretations. However, exactly how difficult is it to find the right materials and replicate the primary sonic qualities of those preeminent pickups today? We asked a few questions to some winders and in the following pages are their sometimes contrasting opinions on "P.A.F." related matters. While the questions were the same for all of them, the length and substance of their answers varied depending on their attitudes, beliefs and personalities.

We are very grateful for their contributions and for accepting the challenge to share with us their experience, knowledge and unique perspectives.

In alphabetical order..we thank you.

# David Bowes
# (Sigil Pickups - www.sigilpickups.com)

What would you describe as the most important qualities of the "Patent Applied For" pickup if you were describing them to someone who has never had the chance to experience an original?

*P.A.F.s are typically clear and punchy but also have this underlying grit to them. Hollow with woody vowel tones that can closely mimic human speech. They sound best clean or with a slight overdrive where the amp just breaks up. Words don't do it justice though, get on YouTube and search "Glen Kuykendall Trainwreck...Can You Hear it Ring" and start at ~1:20 and again at ~2:50. Be sure to use good headphones or speakers!*

In that original P.A.F.s had their own distinct sonic characteristics, and there are quite a few variables to choose from in describing this unique character, what do you think are the most important sonic elements in creating a "historically correct" replica?

*A good P.A.F. replica needs clarity and string separation. Enough brightness without sounding like ice picks in your ears that allow the use of the tone/volume controls. They need to have a range of good tone, not just a one trick wonder.*

Many famous players used P.A.F. equipped guitars. Is there one who represents for you a reference point as far as P.A.F. tone is concerned? Why do you think that player represents a good reference point?

*First and foremost for me is Mike Bloomfield's tone from the Super Sessions album, specifically Albert's Shuffle and Stop. His tone is bright and jangly but you can hear the slightly muffled undertones throughout. My first P.A.F. set (Chicago'68) is a tribute to him and that album. Clapton is another favorite of mine, most notably the Blues Breaker's album. His tone is brooding and moody which is a direct reflection of who he was as a person at the time but is also distinctly a P.A.F. tone. I did the London'66 set in tribute to that album. Peter Green in the original Fleetwood Mac; his tone was ethereal. He had the highly distinctive Out-Of-Phase tone that isn't easy to replicate and became a bit of an obsession for me for quite a while. Modern players, I'm a huge Warren Haynes and Joe Bonamassa fan. Haynes does the vocal guitar sound and has a thick, heavy rolled down tone that I love. Bonamassa takes the Blues/Rock thing to an all new level and is the modern equivalent to the guitar gods of the 60s for me. I actually tried to do up a Bonamassa inspired set a while back but I didn't get there at all. Fortunately, they got me Haynes by accident so I was pleased none the less.*

Today there are many good sounding pickups based on the original P.A.F., but winding methods vary from one winder to the next; for example, some prefer machine winding, some prefer hand winding. Which do you prefer and why?

*I much prefer machine winding. I started with hand winding on a Thomas winding machine which was okay, but I ended up fighting the machine a lot of the time and it ties up your hands which means it's a full commitment to winding a bobbin. I recommend everyone interested in doing it starts this way to get a feel for the whole thing, but after moving to a full machine wind (i.e., auto traverse), I have no desire to go back. I was looking at different machines on eBay for a few months and a 1967 Geo Stevens 39AM came up at a very reasonable price; this was around six months after launching Sigil Pickups. It was in rough shape and really dirty with some missing parts and no guarantee it would work, but I'm okay with intricate machinery so figured I could get it going. I jumped on it and didn't realize just how lucky I got with the purchase until I started researching them. It came with a nearly full set of gears which lets you change the turns per layer; most machines I've seen listed don't have the gears or cams or any of the peripherals. It needed a good cleanup and was missing the faceplate and a suitable cam but had a functional counter and Meteor de-spooler so was mostly complete. I machined an aluminum faceplate for mounting the bobbins, figured out how to design heart shaped cams and 3D printed one then got to figuring it out! The machine is fantastic; so much so that I've added a second Geo to the bench, an earlier model 38 AML. I find that having a good setup on these machines, the wire never snaps so I can let it run while I work on prep for the other parts. The counter has an automatic stop feature so I can set my dials and get what I want. I do a lot of ridiculous turn counts so when I want 4932 turns on a bobbin, I can just set it and go. And yes, I do specify my winds like that...might be a shade of OCD in my builds. Some people say you NEED a machine with auto traverse to get the P.A.F. thing down, but that's a load of BS. It's easier to get good results on an auto traverse but there's no reason a person couldn't do it by hand if they have the determination. I know one guy in particular who was winding some very high-end P.A.F. replicas and was shocked to find out that he was doing it by hand on the same style Thomas winder I started with. His pickups remain among the best I've ever heard. My first 6 months of sales were all hand wound and the reviews were always favorable so I like to think I had something going as well.*

Since so many decades have passed since the original P.A.F.s, how difficult do you feel it is to source suitable materials to make a sonically and historically correct replica?

*Ridiculously difficult at first but it seems to be getting easier the longer I stick around. There are several vendors for parts where I think all people start, but I was finding some stuff was really good and other stuff was not so good from these suppliers. Well, to be fair it's all usable and suitable for building pickups... it's not like they're selling junk, but I'm very particular and want to use the best and most accurate parts for my own peace of mind. I'm not going to package and sell anything that I won't personally use or feel is beneath what I'd expect to get from a reputable winder. It's been a continual search and struggle along the way, mostly in finding proper covers but currently I don't feel I need to change anything. My own costs have gone up considerably and I have to pay shipping from several different places but each piece fits my idea of the perfect P.A.F. so that's just the way it is. Now hopefully the current suppliers I use don't go changing anything or drop out of the scene.*

How would you reply to those who insist that the originals are impossible to match because magnets and wire with the same exact formula and specifications from the past are impossible to find today?

*I'd say they're 10% right... but it's a very hefty 10%. I've acquired numerous vintage parts along the way including some authentic NOS plain enamel wire from the late 50s. I've done personal testing with the old parts compared to the new stuff and there's a distinct difference in the tone with all else being equal, most notably in the wire. My own experience and personal belief is that you can ~90% there with all modern parts. This was what made up the largest part of my myth-busting.*

*When I first got the spool of 1957 PE, I wound up my Chicago set with the wire being the only variant. To my ears it had a deeper tone, not as bright as modern PE and there was a distinctive bloom that to me can best be described as similar to the difference between a solid state and tube amp, but not quite as profound. Solid State amps are fine and can sound great, but when you plug into a tube amp there's just so much more texture to the sound. You can just hear and feel more of the range of the tone which is how the vintage wire reacted... again, it's a lot more subtle than the amp analogy but it's there. I was concerned that I was imagining things so did up some sets that I sent out to people as contest giveaways and some random orders, but I didn't tell them they had the vintage wire. I marked these sets with an 'SE' on the labels and kept track of the new owner's feedback and impressions. They all seemed to find the same things I experienced so it was helpful in letting me know I wasn't just falling into some of the hype that's been spread around. I finished up that wire on my Roots 57 LTD sets and then kept an eye out for any hints of more sources for vintage wire. It's not common, but I got lucky in a few cases over the past couple years when I scored the 1958 spool and several 1959 spools from different places.*

Are there details of the originals which are particularly difficult to get right?

*Covers. Covers have been the bane of my pickup building from the get go. Most suppliers have these cheap looking budget covers that do their job and are decent material, but they're nothing like a genuine P.A.F. cover. Magnets aren't too bad but I found I had to go direct to the manufacturers to get any kind of consistency. Some suppliers do baseplates wrong but I was able to source some really nice ones right away. Bobbins, pole screws and slugs were also not hard to source once I settled on what I wanted. Coil geometry is tricky to figure out but not overly difficult to mimic.*

Is there something in the way the originals were built that you found interesting from a manufacturing point of view? Is there something that surprised or intrigued you?

*The mythology indicates the P.A.F.s were random and uncontrolled but I have a hard time believing they'd leave the main influence on the tone of the Les Paul to chance. That's no way to impress people and sell a product. It just makes no sense to me that they'd go through all the trouble of developing and filing the patent just to mindlessly throw them together. It was a large operation with a lot of people making them on different machines with different wire spools which accounts for the inconsistencies from one pickup to the next but there had to be guidelines and some kind of QC going on despite what people claim to know. As far as how they're constructed no, there's nothing overly surprising in how they were built. Breaking down the mechanics of a P.A.F. or any pickup, they're really simple devices.*

Do you use fully charged magnets or magnets charged to a given strength to get vintage tones? Is there a certain type of AlNiCo that you prefer to work with?

*I have no preference and use whatever AlNiCo blend sounds best in each pickup, typically I have a specific magnet in mind when I design the coil geometry but I test each type to see which fits best. As for charging, I use both fully charged and deGaussed. For P.A.F. winds, my Chicago'68 set uses full charged AlNiCo IV; the London '66 uses full A4 neck and deGaussed A5 bridge (Thanks E.C. for the suggestion there); Bootlegs use full charged A5 in both; Roots 57 use full A3 in both; Black Magic is full A2 and A3; my latest 1959 Wire 'Holy Grail' sets are using A2 neck and vintage spec deGaussed A5 bridge. From the 1958 wire I wound a set and am liking full A5 in the bridge with A2 coming in a close second and A4 in the neck but those aren't final yet. I bought some monstrous N52 magnets for charging when I got started and did a lot of testing of Gauss at different levels from as low as 10% to see the effect. I keep a notebook that's pretty much my own personal Bible of all this testing and comments on impressions.*

Do you offer repair/restoration services?

*Yes I do! I prefer to build my own but I'm always willing to help people get their pickups back in working order. I'm always open to custom ideas and have done quite a few interesting and off the wall sets. I love the P.A.F. but I'm not purely stuck on it.*

# Jon Gundry
# (Throbak Electronics - www.throbak.com)

What would you describe as the most important qualities of the "Patent Applied For" pickup if you were describing them to someone who has never had the chance to experience an original?

*Clarity and wide dynamic response are what I consider to be the most distinctive tonal attributes of a P.A.F. The P.A.F. is very responsive to pick dynamics and guitar volume pot adjustment. And whether a warmer or brighter P.A.F., there is an inherent clarity to the individual notes that is a hallmark of the P.A.F.*

In that original P.A.F.s had their own distinct sonic characteristics, and there are quite a few variables to choose from in describing this unique character, what do you think are the most important sonic elements in creating a "historically correct" replica?

*A vintage P.A.F. has treble overtones in both the wound and unwound strings that are particularly noticeable if the pickup has been unpotted. The character of these treble overtones changes with steel and magnet chemistry and winding specs. For me, making a P.A.F. pre-production that has this extra level of tonal complexity in treble content is essential.*

Many famous players used P.A.F. equipped guitars. Is there one who represents for you a reference point as far as P.A.F. tone is concerned? Why do you think that player represents a good reference point?

*Peter Green I think demonstrated the level of dynamic response that a P.A.F. can reproduce in a way that few others have come close to. His use of volume and even tone pot adjustment as well as the out-of-phase P.A.F. tone is incredible when you listen to his live recordings. Eric Clapton showed everyone the power and punch a Les Paul with P.A.F.s can have and Paul Kossoff revealed the almost orchestral chordal quality a P.A.F. is capable of. And Albert King showed them all that a guitar with P.A.F. pickups can sing in the hands of a master.*

Today there are many good sounding pickups based on the original P.A.F., but winding methods vary from one winder to the next; for example, some prefer machine winding, some prefer hand winding. Which do you prefer and why?

*I guess I'm a purist when it comes to machine winding a P.A.F. At ThroBak we make a P.A.F. reproduction in the purest sense of the word. I take great efforts to duplicate every aspect of a vintage P.A.F. including the machine winding process. All vintage P.A.F. pickups were machine wound, that's a fact. And tonally there is a real difference between a machine wound and hand wound pickup. In general terms you get a more defined low end with a machine wound pickup. There are many people striving to make a P.A.F. repro, with many different approaches. Some hand guide the wire, some machine guide the wire, some even leave parts out of the original P.A.F. assembly. These are all valid choices for individual pickup makers. But for me, I have to have my P.A.F. repros machine wound with a complete P.A.F. pickup assembly, with all the details found in vintage P.A.F. pickups.*

Since so many decades have passed since the original P.A.F.s, how difficult do you feel it is to source suitable materials to make a sonically and historically correct replica?

*Sourcing the correct materials and parts for a P.A.F. repro took quite a bit of persistence but that was part of the fun for me. I had to be informed about what I needed which required investment in lab tests of vintage parts and meetings with parts makers to nail down specs. It took a lot of time and a lot of research. Luckily many of the shops that once supplied Gibson Kalamazoo are still here in the Midwest which helped quite a bit in finding people with the knowledge and history to make historically correct parts.*

How would you reply to those who insist that the originals are impossible to match because magnets and wire with the same exact formula and specifications from the past are impossible to find today?

*Vintage AlNiCo magnets can absolutely be accurately duplicated but I don't think I could have done without using USA magnet makers. The USA magnet makers have processes and records that go back many decades. The metal mix of a vintage magnet can be found and duplicated with the same materials. However variations in heat treating processes also have a tonal impact on a guitar pickup magnet. USA magnet makers have specific knowledge going back decades as it relates to magnets in guitar pickups. You just don't get that level of history and knowledge with overseas magnet makers.*

*As far as magnet wire goes I can get the full vintage range of ohms per foot and wire diameter within the 42AWG tolerance. Tonally the ohms per foot relative to wire diameter is what impacts the tone of a P.A.F. whether vintage or a repro.*

Are there details of the originals which are particularly difficult to get right?

*I did find it frustrating that I could not find 1016 steel. However the specs for 1016 cross over with 1018 which meant that I could find 1018 batches with 1016 specs. It made it difficult but not impossible to get the keeper bar specs correct. It was also a challenge to find screw makers willing to run pole screws with the lower carbon content required for vintage accurate specs. Most all screw manufacturers would only quote screws with 1022 steel which is not a vintage correct spec. But again persistence goes a long way towards making an accurate P.A.F. reproduction.*

*Also when it came to cosmetics of the P.A.F. bobbin mold I had to make 3 versions of the mold to get the look correct. Luckily my plastic molder is also a muscle car restorer and he understood that the cosmetics matter in a reproduction and was happy to make adjustments as needed.*

Is there something in the way the originals were built that you found interesting from a manufacturing point of view? Is there something that surprised or intrigued you?

*There are quite a few things that I found interesting about how vintage P.A.F.s were manufactured. For example I did not realize how much the grinding and buffing process impacted the look of a P.A.F. cover until I saw it being done first hand. I was also amazed by how much detail about the original bobbin manufacturing my plastic molder could glean an original part. How the magnets were charged and how they were installed in a vintage P.A.F. has an impact on the tone. Variations in start leads of vintage P.A.F.s impacts tone. There are other details like these that are important to address when making a P.A.F. reproduction.*

Do you use fully charged magnets or magnets charged to a given strength to get vintage tones? Is there a certain type of AlNiCo that you prefer to work with?

*It depends on the model of pickup as to whether the magnet is block charged, fully charged or degaussed. Gibson block charged their AlNiCo magnets and when you do this most of the magnets do not get fully saturated with a charge. This leaves some of the magnets prone to losing some charge in a pickup like a P 90 but not so much in a P.A.F. However the magnet may not have been fully saturated because it was block charged. So it really depends on what I'm going for tonally as to the level of charge and how I accomplish it. Also I use old formulation magnets and even fully saturated they do not charge as high as overseas made magnets.*

*Personally, just speaking as a guitar player, I prefer A2 and A5 for a P.A.F. and A4, A2 and A3 for a P 90. Really I think this comes down to individual player preference.*

Do you offer repair/restoration services?

*I do offer repair and restoration services for vintage P.A.F.s and P 90s. Customers can visit the ThroBak website and get an idea of the full scope of vintage accurate capabilities we have. For a restoration or a rewind I can honestly say we offer a unique and unmatched service. If you have a vintage pickup in need of repair, follow the email link on the ThroBak website and let me know what you need done.*

# Jason Lollar
# (Lollar Pickups - www.lollarguitars.com)

What would you describe as the most important qualities of the "Patent Applied For" pickup if you were describing them to someone who has never had the chance to experience an original?

*The best P.A.F.s have good clarity, note separation, punch and fairly even frequency response. They have enough output where they feel like you are not having to struggle to get decent sustain - a smoother attack than most single coils without the dry feeling lower output pickups can have.*

In that original P.A.F.s had their own distinct sonic characteristics, and there are quite a few variables to choose from in describing this unique character, what do you think are the most important sonic elements in creating a "historically correct" replica?

*The even frequency response is really important - no big hump at any particular frequency and a smoother attack avoiding muddiness though and without any annoying spikes particularly in the higher frequencies. You want some smoothness but you also should get a decent amount of cut so you can come through a mix.*

Many famous players used P.A.F. equipped guitars. Is there one who represents for you a reference point as far as P.A.F. tone is concerned? Why do you think that player represents a good reference point?

*The thing about P.A.F.s is that they were made early on so they were in place to become a defining tone. You can name many players from the 50s to the early 70s that used P.A.F.s and even to today although it would be more common to run across P.A.F.s on earlier recordings. Peter Frampton in Humble Pie, Jimmy Page, Peter Green, Joe Walsh, Duane Allman, Jeff Beck, Martin Barre, Mike Bloomfield, Billy Gibbons - you can go on and on. To pick one out and say they have the definitive tone would be almost funny. Also it's really tough to point to a recording because hearing it first hand is different and so much of what a pickup does is tactile and more noticeable to the player than the typical listener.*

Today there are many good sounding pickups based on the original P.A.F., but winding methods vary from one winder to the next; for example, some prefer machine winding, some prefer hand winding. Which do you prefer and why?

*Originals were machine wound. There is wide spread misinformation about machine wound vs hand wound coils and also differences that are not widely known. It's touted that hand wound always sounds superior to machine wound which I find not to be true. The dogma is that machine wound coils have each turn perfectly aligned next to each other which supposedly sounds inferior to hand winding. In practice even a very accurate programmable machine will start to oscillate while winding the coil in a way that will lay the wire randomly to some extent. The amount the wire gets off track can vary to an extreme depending on how the machine is set up. The result at best is with an oblong coil like a guitar pickup you never get a perfectly parallel winding pattern with the same amount of turns per layer and if your intent is to get more of a scatter pattern you can achieve various amounts of that with more consistency from coil to coil than you could do by hand winding. A coil made with more turns per layer will have higher inductance than one with less turns - (with some exceptions) - so you can get a clear sound with more output to drive the amp with, where a more scattered coil – (hand wound)- you can get a clear sound with a cleaner signal and a punchier attack. That said it is possible to get contradicting results if you really push the variables to their extremes. Generally if you are trying to get a tonality people expect out of a humbucker you will want to use an auto winder. The auto winders I use are very old mechanical winders designed in the 30s or 40s, virtually identical internally to almost any early mechanical winder including the fabled Leesona Gibson reportedly used. You can hand wind humbuckers and come out with good results but you can get more output and grind without having to pile on as much wire. It can be a subtle difference to most but once you hear it the difference becomes more obvious.*

Since so many decades have passed since the original P.A.F.s, how difficult do you feel it is to source suitable materials to make a sonically and historically correct replica?

*I started making pickups in the late 70s and over that time there have been a lot of changes. There are very few AlNiCo magnets still made in the USA. Even up until the late 90's you could find new old stock USA made humbucker magnets left over from runs made for Gibson and other manufacturers. I was told most of the machinery to make AlNiCo was sold off and shipped over to China, same thing with the fiberboard used to make fender pickups. Anyway magnets made now have a lot fewer flaws than what we use to get. I use to throw out about 25% of our magnets due to inclusions and voids so the consistency is usually better. I have found AlNiCo so badly made from the 50s where it wouldn't take a charge properly, it would either not charge up much at all or it wouldn't hold a charge. One of the big problems was the parts suppliers didn't use to sell pickup making parts to the general public or even small shops until around 2000. Since then the whole scenario has changed. I remember up until maybe almost 10 years ago USA companies were not interested in making metal pickup covers, we would get bids of 20,000 dollars to have a deep draw multi step die made so most small makers were and many still are dependent on purchasing from the general guitar parts suppliers and most of what they have is Korean or Chinese made, sometimes Japanese and of course there are some German parts. Anyway we bought direct from Korea and some of their parts are worthy to use but the big problem we had was consistency, particularly on anything that needed polished and plated like the humbucker cover. You would get variation in materials thickness and alloy, variation in the quality of stamping and polishing, variation in the thickness of the plating, variation in how easily the covers would make eddy currents, same goes with pole pieces and a number of parts. Back when the economy went south – 2007 or so - US manufacturers became more agreeable to make parts. I hooked up with a company that makes parts for the guitar industry and they were willing to make a number of parts to my drawings for very little investment on our part. In exchange they allow me exclusive use of these parts for a short period of time then later they can sell these parts to other suppliers and companies. This allowed us to have made*

*thunderbird bass covers, Gibson sized Filter Tron covers, Teisco parts - Fender wide range bucker parts, a number of items that you'll now see many other pickup companies using. The consistency of these parts is impeccable - it's really made a huge difference for everyone.*
*The alloy you choose to have each part made from has a lot to do with the overall tone so consistency in alloy and plating is very important if you want to have known and consistent results. Finding out what the original alloys were requires getting some original spare parts and you can get them analyzed fairly easily at a reasonable cost. For many of the parts used in pickups made after the late 40s you can still get the same alloys. Some of the older metals no longer correspond to modern alloys often due to industry structural standards, anyway if you are willing to get 20 or 50,000 screws made of a particular alloy it's doable. Nickle silver has been a bit hard to get from time to time - this is used for a lot of pickup covers and baseplates but that's just a supply problem.*
*Another problem is even the original pickups used various alloys from batch to batch so you have inconsistency there! The coil wire is generally made to a slightly different specification than it was decades ago and the insulation of the wire is different. Basically what you have to do is have your parts made for you- we even have our coil wire made and even the lead wire is made for us in the USA. That said I have seen plenty of people use extremely close parts bordering on the obsessive where even some tooling marks are copied and they still miss the mark.*
*To me the most important thing is how it sounds - sure you want the appearance to be right but I concentrate more on results than appearance. However, everything we make is flawless so I don't mean appearance as far as having a perfect product. I know of a company that uses the original winding machine Gibson used, they have all the parts made so they have all of the original flaws and they still don't hit the nail on the head. I can only say that because we purchase other companies products just to listen to and compare to the user reviews and forum comments - what you read doesn't always make sense.*

How would you reply to those who insist that the originals are impossible to match because magnets and wire with the same exact formula and specifications from the past are impossible to find today?

*Well you can make a very good pickup with common off the shelve parts if you have experience and even if you don't you can still hit the target sometimes but going beyond and above and having consistency would be very difficult. My thing is and always has been to examine original vintage pickups, assess the strengths and weakness in performance and construction and at first try to match it and then try to surpass it. There are plenty of problems with vintage pickups as far as consistency and there are problems with original materials and construction methods that can affect longevity. For instance the plastic used on the molded P 90 bobbins starting around the late 50s has problems with stability much like speaker surround foam rot so we hand make all of our bobbins out of forbon and glue them together from separate parts like the P 90s from the 1940s which never rot. We also use eyelets like a fender pickup to attach the lead wires to the coil wires, this makes a better strain proof connection and it makes the pickup easier to service and it will outlive anything Gibson made since the 40s. What's that saying - they don't make them like they use to? Well we make them better than they use to any time it's possible.*

Are there details of the originals which are particularly difficult to get right?

*I listened to a lot of P.A.F.s over the years and there is a lot of variation, some just don't sound that good - I don't recall hearing one that sounded bad but I have heard several where it was pretty obvious they didn't keep up with what we make. Now every once in a while you'll get one where it's like – WOW – what's going on here? The last one I played recently like that was a gold top and the neck pickup was like- ahh its nothing special - but the bridge had something going on with the level of microphonics it had and maybe the alloy of the pickup cover - I'm not sure but you could hear these very loud and prominent harmonic overtones which I have heard before on occasion - almost like the percussion setting on a Hammond. Very interesting. I believe it could get in your way at times and it may be annoying if it was always like that in both neck and bridge at that level. I have never heard anyone making P.A.F.s that have managed to replicate that phenomenon and can't think of any recordings where you would hear it either.*

Is there something in the way the originals were built that you found interesting from a manufacturing point of view? Is there something that surprised or intrigued you?

*Not really, by the time they made the P.A.F. designs had become somewhat homogenized - there are a lot more interesting designs from much earlier. I am always looking for ways to improve on construction and reliability, now that 50+ years have gone by its very apparent what aging does to the reliability of vintage pickups. Certain types of plastics degrade and fail, glues and waxes all age. One thing we do different is we use heat shrink tubing over and solder joints where Gibson just folded a piece of paper tape over them. I have seen solder joints work their way through tape over time most likely due to vibration or constant pressure. I believe heat shrink is far more resistant to that. Overall methods used to assemble P.A.F.s were pretty well thought out and reliable. Butyrate used in the bobbins shrinks so the pole pieces will get out of alignment and bind so we use a different type of plastic except for restorations.*

Do you use fully charged magnets or magnets charged to a given strength to get vintage tones? Is there a certain type of AlNiCo that you prefer to work with?

*I use both fully charged and partially deGaussed magnets depending on the result I am after and I use a number of AlNiCo formulations from Al 2 to Al 8. On the pickups we intend to sound most like a P.A.F. the magnets are deGaussed to specific levels and we use very accurate Gauss meters that will measure down to two decimal points. AlNiCo bar magnets typically measure in the hundreds so in the range of 420 to 820 depending on the grade and if it's fully charged or not.*

Do you offer repair/restoration services?

*Yes we will take in that sort of repair work if we have an opening in our schedule and as far as P.A.F.s go we try to do a repair so you would not be able to see anyone had been inside it or changed anything if someone wants that level of detail, which generally they do.*

# Wolfe Mcleod
# (WolfeTone Pickups - www.wolfetone.com)

What would you describe as the most important qualities of the "Patent Applied For" pickup if you were describing them to someone who has never had the chance to experience an original?

*Liveliness and touch sensitivity. They should never sound like they have a blanket put over the speaker.*

In that original P.A.F.s had their own distinct sonic characteristics, and there are quite a few variables to choose from in describing this unique character, what do you think are the most important sonic elements in creating a "historically correct" replica?

*Most people think that P.A.F.s were very warm and creamy, but in reality, they had a nice top-end bite to them, almost like a Telecaster. It's hard to nail down one characteristic though, since they were all over the map. If I had to though, I would say that liveliness would be the single most important characteristic. As far as creating "historically correct" replicas, I feel that many people are spending too much time and money to create a perfect visual replica, but not enough attention to tonal qualities.*

Many famous players used P.A.F. equipped guitars. Is there one who represents for you a reference point as far as P.A.F. tone is concerned? Why do you think that player represents a good reference point?

*Hard to pick just one! I'd have to pick two... Duane Allman and Jimmy Page, because they were on opposite ends of the spectrum.*

Today there are many good sounding pickups based on the original P.A.F., but winding methods vary from one winder to the next; for example, some prefer machine winding, some prefer hand winding. Which do you prefer and why?

*Since hand-winding of humbucker coils can lead to odd resonances, I tend to prefer machine wound, especially since vintage P.A.F.s were not hand-wound. Machine winding also gives greater consistency, and contrary to popular belief, there are machines that can radically scatter coils in a desired fashion.*

Since so many decades have passed since the original P.A.F.s, how difficult do you feel it is to source suitable materials to make a sonically and historically correct replica?

*It is getting quite difficult. Magnet materials have changed over the decades. Older AlNiCo has been shown to be purer, with fewer pollutants in the metals, so to speak. Newer AlNiCo is less pure. I think this is stemming from the repeated recycling of aluminum which may lead to impurities. When it comes to coil wire, certain ingredients such as benzene and lead seem to have been removed from the insulation. This changes dielectric constants and alters the flow of electrons.*

How would you reply to those who insist that the originals are impossible to match because magnets and wire with the same exact formula and specifications from the past are impossible to find today?

*I would have to say that they are correct, for the most part.*

Are there details of the originals which are particularly difficult to get right?

*No difficulties in the way they were built, that's pretty straightforward. But, those sonic characteristics have proven a challenge for everyone, due to the lack of proper and higher purity materials. We can get close, though.*

Is there something in the way the originals were built that you found interesting from a manufacturing point of view? Is there something that surprised or intrigued you?

*I always wondered why Gibson chose to thread the adjustable screw-holes in the base-plates. That's a PITA to deal with during assembly.*

Do you use fully charged magnets or magnets charged to a given strength to get vintage tones? Is there a certain type of AlNiCo that you prefer to work with?

*I use both full strength and slightly deGaussed magnets. I tend to lean towards AlNiCo 2 for my P.A.F. style pickups.*

Do you offer repair/restoration services?

*Yes, we sure do.*

# Tim Mills (BareKnucklePickups-www.bareknucklepickups.co.uk)

What would you describe as the most important qualities of the "Patent Applied For" pickup if you were describing them to someone who has never had the chance to experience an original?

*Clarity, note definition, dynamic control and harmonic overtones. When you play a great vintage P.A.F. there really is no tone like it on earth. They really are extremely versatile pickups, you can play virtually any style with them.*

In that original P.A.F.s had their own distinct sonic characteristics, and there are quite a few variables to choose from in describing this unique character, what do you think are the most important sonic elements in creating a "historically correct" replica?

*In terms of tone, the most important qualities for me are dynamics and note 'bloom'. A good P.A.F. (and not all of them sounded good by a long way) will feel like it is literally trying to talk as you play because they are so dynamically responsive to your touch. Notes should erupt or bloom from under your fingers. It's an extremely vocal tone and feels like the guitar is talking through you.*

Many famous players used P.A.F. equipped guitars. Is there one who represents for you a reference point as far as P.A.F. tone is concerned? Why do you think that player represents a good reference point?

*There are many, many great tonal references for P.A.F. tone and it would be hard to pick just one player. From back in the day Peter Green, Eric Clapton, Duane Allman, Paul Kossoff and Jimmy Page through to more modern players like Gary Moore and Joe Bonamassa, who was arguably a huge exponent of P.A.F. tone with his collection of vintage LPs.*

*As far as tonal reference goes, I feel that it does lean very much towards your own musical preferences when it comes to choosing iconic players. I've always based my own versions of P.A.F.s on the best original P.A.F.s I have been fortunate to playtest as I feel that's more objective in recreating the dynamic feel of the original humbucker.*

Today there are many good sounding pickups based on the original P.A.F., but winding methods vary from one winder to the next; for example, some prefer machine winding, some prefer hand winding. Which do you prefer and why?

*I hand wind all my coils. It's all I've ever done, it's the only way I know and it works for my customers and me.*

*Although it generally takes longer to do than an automated, pre-tensioned machine winder I'm dedicated to hand winding as I believe it produces a better tone from the finished pickups. In fact, it is very much the tone of Bare Knuckle and I wouldn't want to change that as it's the bench mark of all Bare Knuckle pickups.*

Since so many decades have passed since the original P.A.F.s, how difficult do you feel it is to source suitable materials to make a sonically and historically correct replica?

*So long as you've done your research correctly it's not difficult. Like all things, it just takes hard work. We tooled up many years ago and produce all of our components in-house to guarantee they're 100% vintage accurate: celluloid butyrate bobbins, 21AWG nickel silver baseplates, covers made from solid German nickel silver, pole shoes, slugs, fillister screws, right down to hand-cut maple spacers.*

How would you reply to those who insist that the originals are impossible to match because magnets and wire with the same exact formula and specifications from the past are impossible to find today?

*You can recreate anything if you spend enough time and effort. In the end, most importantly, you're recreating not just a physical object but a tone. Tone is very subjective so ultimately you have to make that decision and produce what you believe to be the most tonally accurate P.A.F. based on original examples you have playtested for comparison.*

Are there details of the originals which are particularly difficult to get right?

*There's a lot of work that goes into getting the tooling for the parts correct. Getting the right draw in the corners of covers and around the pole screw holes took a lot of work with constant referencing to the best original examples. The baseplate tooling also involved a lot of work - getting the right angles in the mounting leg and tab, right down to the grain of the nickel silver and original tooling marks.*

Is there something in the way the originals were built that you found interesting from a manufacturing point of view? Is there something that surprised or intrigued you?

*The very first prototype P.A.F.s had two slug coils, the screw coil former came a little later, so despite the same tool maker being used for both, the tooling for each former is slightly different. In particular the internal dimensions of the island in the center of the bobbin which the wire is wound around. This is crucial in replicating the original formers correctly and extremely important to the final tone.*

Do you use fully charged magnets or magnets charged to a given strength to get vintage tones? Is there a certain type of AlNiCo that you prefer to work with?

*It depends on the AlNiCo. I use fully charged AlNiCo V and specifically charged AlNiCo II, III and IV, all rough cast. I have a personal preference for AlNiCo IV when it comes to P.A.F.s but I offer a range of P.A.F. models that covers AII through to AV.*

Do you offer repair/restoration services?

*Yes I do. I have repaired many original P.A.F.s over the years, double whites, double blacks and the odd zebra too (yes they do exist!).*

# Dave Stephens
# (Stephens Design Pickups - www.sdpickups.com)

What would you describe as the most important qualities of the "Patent Applied For" pickup if you were describing them to someone who has never had the chance to experience an original?

*This is a hard question to answer. I have read all kinds of flowery descriptions about "genuine P.A.F. tone", stuff like "bloom", and "double notes", but neither of those two things are accurate in my view. Double notes happen only certain places on the neck and usually with brighter pickups. They come from the fact there are two coils, each one hearing a different part of the string, it's that simple, and it happens mostly at certain areas on the neck. Any "bucker" can do it and it's not magic. "Bloom", again I don't think this comes from the pickup, I think it comes from low magnetic power pickups, which P.A.F.s definitely are. And from how loud your amp is turned up. They say it's when you play a note, it gets a little louder before dying. This is a sign of the amp interacting with the magnet pull on the string I think. You play a note, the string pull is low so the string can vibrate more freely, it subtly is being sustained by amp output, so there is a slight rise, then it dies off. It's really a simple type of compressor effect with the amp and pickups. Could be wrong but that's what I think.*

*First of all, they are brighter than anyone thinks they are who have never played one. The reason this surprises people is because they are listening to old Zeppelin, or the "Beano" album, or any of that stuff. Never forget those albums were recorded on analog tape, using tube driven studio gear, compression and often plate reverb, with vintage tube amps, higher capacitance vintage guitar coil cords, and a studio engineer who almost always dialed down the treble EQ and tailored the sound of the guitar to sound "good". The proof of this is Clapton's "Beano" tone. You have to listen to the VINYL version and only the MONO version first. Then listen to the stereo version and you notice right away the guitar sounds much less raw. Then go find Mayall's "Primal Solos" album that he recorded with a voice microphone on a portable tape recorder at their live gigs. Now you hear Eric's guitar is way brighter and more raw and biting in the live non-studio version. So, all my customers who actually acquire a vintage P.A.F. or guitar with original installed P.A.F.s, tell me "I can't believe how bright these are, I actually have to use my tone controls". Pretty funny.*

*All those classic players used their tone controls a lot! That shows up in the studio recordings too. It's a mistake to copy a recorded sound, you must copy the device, not something from an audio engineer's head.*

*So, they are bright, they have a single coil kind of sound to me, but it's fatter because you got two coils and sets of poles hearing two different parts of the string, which always fattens up the sound. They are almost never harsh though, but they can verge just inches away from being so sometimes. They have a "vocal" quality that's hard to describe. On the Beano album, "All Your Love" in the very opening lick, sliding two notes quickly up the neck, you can hear it's a full bodied "wowww" kind of sound. Solos, "talk", more vocally than say a Telecaster can. There is a "sweetness" to them in high notes, that can be violin-like at times but still very bright. With tone controls all the way off, the "woman tone" thing, its a delicious kind of soda pop fizzing sound I can't begin to describe, it's not muddy. Some of that though is from the ultra simple transparent harnesses from the good parts that were used on the old guitars.*

*To me they are like a very fine wine. If you don't know wine, the cheapest wine and the most expensive wines are indistinguishable from each other, because an educated taste has not been developed. In modern times, there's two guys who have really carried the torch for vintage P.A.F. tones, Gary Moore, and Joe Bonamassa (I'm not really a fan of his, but he knows how to use these guitars). J.D. Simo is another guy I've seen on YouTube who knows how to use them properly. Bonamassa uses too many amps and rack mount stuff and pedals but he keeps it pretty pure. There's a few more guys like that out there. My favorite vintage player for his P.A.F. 'burst tones was Peter Green. He seems to have preferred Fender amps and I do too. Very beautiful passionate solos, pure P.A.F. sweetness, low distortion, good headroom amps.*

In that original P.A.F.s had their own distinct sonic characteristics, and there are quite a few variables to choose from in describing this unique character, what do you think are the most important sonic elements in creating a "historically correct" replica?

*What's most important in creating an accurate P.A.F. replica? Absolute fidelity to the true technical details and materials of the original pickups. Period. Copy the technical device, not the "sound".*

*You can't "wind" this sound into existence. And the winding of real P.A.F.s was a strict machine auto wind and one pattern. Never hand wound; hand winding is death to pure P.A.F. sound.*

*A vintage P.A.F. is a technical device of times gone by. I was seven years old when they started using them on guitars, I guess that makes me vintage too. My entire approach was a reverse-engineering effort. I didn't try to recreate "that sound". I tried to recreate the technical device, every microscopic part of materials, physical design, the "soul" was a result of getting everything right. There is no single "secret" that will give you those tones, they are a sum of every single part and materials. You simply cannot isolate one thing out, you can't focus on getting the sound only, the sum creates more than the whole. If one thing is wrong, the whole never works.*
*I first went after the magnetic circuit metallurgy, and it was way way more complex than I could have ever dreamt. But that doesn't get you there. The design itself wasn't consistent from year to year, the materials themselves were changing year by year and eventually the modernizing of materials is what killed them in the end. You must not make "improvements", you must remain true to what they actually ARE, warts and all. This is why the big companies fail, they listen to records, not to real P.A.F.s. They chase a more "pleasing" sound than P.A.F.s ever were. The other thing I forgot to mention, is that there's a few parts sellers out there now, selling "P.A.F. accurate" parts. Whenever I see them pop up, I buy them and check them out. So far, none of any of it is right. So, that's why I produce so few pickups. I make things in real small batches in my skimpy machine shop, do all my own plating, anything I can do or make myself I will and will do them as close as humanly possible*

*to look and sound like real vintage parts. I'm at heart a true technical nerd and I love machines and fabrication. I had a stint as an art jeweler metalsmith back in the 90s and it taught me a lot about constructing things and using those kinds of tools, many of which I still have and use.*

*All I know about them is from proving my ideas to myself thru countless experiments and direct head to head comparisons to real vintage P.A.F.s in my guitars, in person. I use unforgiving vintage Fender amps that quickly show me if the tiniest thing is off.*

*I also took all the magnetic circuits parts sold by all the sellers and had them analyzed, nothing was P.A.F. correct. So, you asked a simple question but the answer is long and involved. Vintage P.A.F.s were my "Master Teachers". They taught me about all vintage pickups, a vast amount of knowledge.*

Many famous players used P.A.F. equipped guitars. Is there one who represents for you a reference point as far as P.A.F. tone is concerned? Why do you think that player represents a good reference point?

*Peter Green and Michael Bloomfield are my 2 favorite "reference" players. Both played a lot thru Fender amps, not small 6V6 powered amps. The small amps just don't mostly have the right head-room, they break up too fast. I have a vintage Princeton and my vintage P.A.F.s sound horrible in that amp, harsh, just bad. The big Fender amps used 6L6 power tubes, they break up just right and have the right headroom and no super distorted sounds. This is also why I like the JTM45s, they were basically a Bassman with KT66s which is another good power tube for the same reasons. In video you see Peter using Showmans a lot, Bloomfield really liked his Twin Reverb with JBL's, those JBL's have a special sound. Most players don't know that Bloomfield used 12 or 13 gauge strings, probably Black Diamonds which all of us were stuck with in the 60s, there were no light gauge strings until the early 70s. We didn't know that British players like Clapton and Page were buying light banjo strings and replacing the G B and high E strings with them and not using the heavy bass strings from the heavy sets. I never even heard of this until many years later. Bloomfield also used Super Reverbs. I love this because the sound is clear, not heavy distortion which masks any subtleties, or dynamics, and soul.*
*Even Clapton's Beano album, it was a JTM45, with more pure sound.*

*But, I looked at all the classic players in detail. Jimmy Page, Jeff Beck, Keith Richards, Duane Allman especially, a long list.*

Today there are many good sounding pickups based on the original P.A.F., but winding methods vary from one winder to the next; for example, some prefer machine winding, some prefer hand winding. Which do you prefer and why?

*No Gibson pickup, from all the vintage models they ever made during the 40-year time span that I dissected vintage examples, was ever hand wound. So, let's look at magnet wire insulations and other aspects of coil winding; insulation coatings have a "dielectric" effect, in other words, how efficient an insulator each type of insulation is. Formvar is less effective an insulator so formvar wire kills more treble, than plain enamel. "Output" is actually determined by how many turns of wire around the coil there are. One turn equals one unit of voltage. Doesn't matter how big or small the turn is, it puts out the same voltage as long as it's in the same strength of magnetic field. Coils are super complex things in physics terms, way beyond quantifying by measuring instruments. Then it gets more complex when you get into winding patterns. Machine automated wound coils pretty much put each turn of wire up against the last turn of wire. As soon as you put one wind of wire a distance away from the last turn, now you have a "scatter" wind, even though it still an automatic wind. So "scatter winding" is not hand winding exclusively. So with single coils, it's why Leo Fender taught his girls a specific way to wind their coils, and Gibson used book formulas to choose their patterns with P.A.F.s and all their pickups. But a very early '57 P.A.F. I restored had the same pattern as P 90s of that year. And probably later in the year it changed to the winding pattern that was used on all P.A.F.s and all Patent Numbers. It was the only exception I've ever seen.*

*By 1965 the P.A.F. formula quit working, because materials technology advances were making more pure products which made the pickups more harsh, so they had to change the winding pattern drastically in T-Tops, to combat the annoying harshness. Vintage wire is a complex subject, Elektrisola Wire Corp. examined in their lab, vintage plain enamel from all the years of Gibson pickups that we analyzed in the steel lab, (40-year time-span), plus a few from very early Fender pickups as well. They tested for a whole list of qualities that I don't want to go into here. There is the bare wire diameter and insulation thickness measurements, though, this alone tells me a lot about any magnet wire. They use lasers to measure these things because its microscopic measurements. Generally the early P.A.F.s used thicker wire because most 42 gauge wire then was at the upper limits of OD tolerances (outside diameter). The last P.A.F.s used much thinner wire, this is a big change in sound. Early P.A.F.s had long fat magnets, this can be heard. The early magnets were very low power (and no, there were no AlNiCo 3 magnets ever used in P.A.F.s). By '59 the magnets were improving in power and brightness, they began using shorter versions, probably because assembling a humbucker with a long magnet can be difficult to stuff the coils leads into tiny spaces, a short magnet makes assembly much easier. But this too, made a sound change......AlNiCo is about 70% iron, the more iron you have in the mass of a magnet, the more treble is limited because iron sucks up treble frequencies thru eddy currents. Eddy currents are like little whirlpools of electric interference which oppose the flow of current, which limits treble. Making a magnet shorter brightens the sound.*

Since so many decades have passed since the original P.A.F.s, how difficult do you feel it is to source suitable materials to make a sonically and historically correct replica?

*Very difficult to source proper materials for what I do. I can't comment on this too much, as I must protect my work. But materials from different manufacturers are all quite variable. The biggest part of those tones is the magnet wire. It's a big key, and is the biggest reason all vintage pickups sound the way they do, but again, you cannot isolate wire from the rest of the machine, but wire is big in vintage tone.*

*With magnets, there is no such thing as "AlNiCo 2." Every factory makes their own version of it, uses different materials. Vintage magnets don't match any modern magnets in materials, and sound, though some I had made are very close. The same thing with steel, with wire.*

How would you reply to those who insist that the originals are impossible to match because magnets and wire with the same exact formula and specifications from the past are impossible to find today?

*People who say that it is impossible to match vintage materials etc. are mostly right. But I am one who will die falling on my sword to prove that if you use your intellect, your mind, your creativity and analytical reasoning powers, backed up by insatiable curiosity for the things in the world, instead of listening to people who tell you, that "you can't do this", then you are doomed. Plus I had the backing of the world's best technical measuring instruments and mentors who gave freely of their time, time that I never could have paid for. Yes, there are things you cannot copy, you cannot get certain things in a P.A.F. replica unless you have real old crude, crappy, awful, garbage vintage magnet wire. I am never satisfied and always trying to close the tiny gaps, to find some way.*

*No, we cannot recreate those old pickups 100%, it's not possible now. It is possible to get extremely close to those old pickups, but oh man, it wore me out finding out how to do it. The world today is about mass production, high profits, high overstated marketing slogans that seldom have any truth to them. But this is not new. When I was 22 years old Gibson told the world they were going to give us the Les Paul again, which had ceased being produced about 1961, it was now 1972 and they gave us a plywood sandwich with mini-humbuckers in it, I bought one and it was a terrible guitar. Awful. Junk. I refuse to mass produce "hamburger" pickups. I go to ridiculous extremes to make my replica P.A.F.s as humanly close to the real deal, the "holy grail" that can ever be done.*

Are there details of the originals which are particularly difficult to get right?

*Magnet wire. Not possible to get. I know enough from the Elektrisola lab work and from the Korean wire I bought years ago that it can be made a lot closer, but I don't have $50,000 to do an experiment that has to start at the very beginning of wire making. The old magnet wire had an almost abrasive insulation, the wire would not slip over itself, even if you wind very loose, the insulation makes the coil feel tightly wound when it's not, because the wires cannot slip over each other because of the near abrasive insulation. The old wire, no matter how loose you wind it, makes coils that feel very tightly wound, it's because the wire is not slippery. The plain enamel wire we get now is the same bare wire that is coated with other insulations, but it's way different than what happened in the 50s, it would be a major undertaking to make this kind of wire again and we have pollution laws that prevent the use of benzene and other things that make this a seriously expensive project. It can be done, but I'm just an old guy that can't do this by myself.*

Is there something in the way the originals were built that you found interesting from a manufacturing point of view? Is there something that surprised or intrigued you?

*All of it. My P.A.F. research also included all of the others, P 13s, Charlie Christian, P 90s, P.A.F. mini-buckers (in Epiphones only and have P.A.F. decals on them) P.A.F.s of course, early Patents, early T-Tops and late T-Tops. They are all very interesting and I have dissected all of them and tested the metals and know about the wire used in them all. Magnet wire and steel are two big stories and so important in all those pickups, and the wire varied from the earlier pickups to the later ones. All of it intrigued me. I saw them try radically different things, like varnishing magnets in P 13s to electrically isolate them from the baseplate. Shims, taped magnets. The beauty of early Gibson work was they were a craftsman workshop. Not a big ass factory with a CEO who only cares about profits more than history. It's also why you never find two vintage Les Pauls that are identical, even though those tops were basically carved by a machine and finished by hand. Even within the short years P.A.F.s were made, you see that technologies back then and especially Gibson's use of the cheapest suppliers they could find, made for radically inconsistent parts making. Plus materials technologies were rapidly changing in those short years, these newer technologies are what killed the P.A.F. recipe. Steel making and wire making and AlNiCo magnet making "improved" but these were detrimental to P.A.F. sound. The last of the Patent pickups became shrill, horrible harsh treble. I have had some '64 Patents in here that showed me the P.A.F. idea was dead. These examples were the worst pickups you would ever want to play, they were so harsh and bright.*

Do you use fully charged magnets or magnets charged to a given strength to get vintage tones? Is there a certain type of AlNiCo that you prefer to work with?

*I never charge my magnets more than what vintage P.A.F.s had in them. I measure every P.A.F. magnet right away that I pull from a P.A.F. They also immediately lose strength once they are outside their assembly. All these magnets are very weak compared to now. I also recharge the vintage ones to see what the max amount of charge they can hold is, it's about 100 Gauss difference, and they always will revert to low readings because AlNiCo in those days was very low tech. Also Gibson always bought the cheapest magnets they could get and even "rejected" magnets to save money. P.A.F. magnets are given way too much credit for those tones, there are no magic magnets.*

Do you offer repair/restoration services?

*Yes I repair, rebuild, restore, bring old P.A.F.s back from the dead all the time, many every year. If someone is rich, I charge them for the work, if some poor musician has one and can't afford it, I fix them for free. This is also my research library, every single old P.A.F. has a story to tell, I know how to read those stories. It's not magic, its science, it is engineering and it takes a pickup designer to know how to read it.*

*This is not cold science, these pickups tell me what they are and I spent a lot of time with originals. They will tell you things if you are so in love with them to look at every thing they show you. I love the art of them, I love the process of cutting steel, nickel plating, testing materials for suitability to stay as close to the real sound as possible, I love this stuff. My relic processes are pure art, years to invent the ways of aging these metals. The materials talk to you, they tell you what they are, if you work with them, you know them.*

*This is my life, which is art, music, love. That's what playing guitar is.*

# Aleksandar Vrhovec
# (Wizz Pickups - www.wizz-pickups.net)

What would you describe as the most important qualities of the "Patent Applied For" pickup if you were describing them to someone who has never had the chance to experience an original?

*The most important quality of the P.A.F. pickup is the sound, the second thing is the looks, and the third thing are the details (like the aging).*

*The original P.A.F. sound is very versatile, very sonic, very mellow, and very sensitive; and when you need it to be aggressive it can do that, too. P.A.F. pickups are probably the most famous pick-ups in the world because they fit all genres, all styles and every individual player's unique sound.*

*P.A.F.s are inspiring and can be considered a 'must have' for the artist behind the guitar. They can also be described as the greatest microphone a guitar player could ever need. They just transform your ideas in the best possible way into music. With them you can play jazz, blues, rock, folk, metal and any modern style you want.*

*The original P.A.F. looks are something I am obsessed with, too, I just can't help myself when looking at them in vintage guitars. They have the perfect design... that's why I have seven sets now.*

*They say the devil is in the details, and that is very true of original P.A.F.s. It is very hard to copy each and every detail, but each detail must be 100% vintage correct. There can be no compromise on replicating and aging them to perfection. I age them so they look like they have been played for 60 years, not just to look rusty.*

In that original P.A.F.s had their own distinct sonic characteristics, and there are quite a few variables to choose from in describing this unique character, what do you think are the most important sonic elements in creating a "historically correct" replica?

*The most important thing to me that they don't have a 'muddy' neck and not an overly shrill/trebly bridge, that is the primary, basic idea.*

*When you do that kind of calibration, images of everything else naturally follow; double tones, woman tone, sustain, bite, etc. This can all be done by correctly replicating the parts and with the correct winding pattern.*

Many famous players used P.A.F. equipped guitars. Is there one who represents for you a reference point as far as P.A.F. tone is concerned? Why do you think that player represents a good reference point?

*Yes, my favorites are Jimmy Page, the Allman Brothers, Billy Gibbons, Eric Clapton and of course, Peter Green. When you hear their records played with P.A.F. equipped guitars it is not possible to remain indifferent. Even if you are not a player, you can hear and feel their soul in their playing.*

*P.A.F.s are the foundations of rock 'n' roll and also the roots of modern rock music.*

Today there are many good sounding pickups based on the original P.A.F., but winding methods vary from one winder to the next; for example, some prefer machine winding, some prefer hand winding. Which do you prefer and why?

*I prefer winding them on my vintage machine from the 1950s. It is a vintage Meteor and I got it in mint condition from Switzerland several years ago.*

*The same brand and model Meteor was also used in the 1950s in the Gibson Kalamazoo plant when winding the original P.A.F. pickups. They had a few other brands of machines, but these were the most durable and they were used on into the 1960s as well. I believe they still have a few of them today.*

Since so many decades have passed since the original P.A.F.s, how difficult do you feel it is to source suitable materials to make a sonically and historically correct replica?

*I think all of the materials are possible to get nowadays with the exception of the wire. Wire just isn't made the same way as it was in the 1950s, but it is very very similar. From time to time I buy vintage wire if I can find it. It is a blessing to work with and sounds amazing.*

*These days, the Internet helps us Europeans connect with American companies to get things done the correct way. We can still get parts from the factories that made them for Gibson in the 1950s (for example, screws, hookup wire, etc.)*

*I make the other stuff with my own tools and molds: bobbins, baseplates, keeper bars, wood spacers, covers, slugs, etc. I even make my own M69 mounting rings, which are 100% identical to the originals (and I give them away for free with every set of P.A.F.s I ship to customers).*

How would you reply to those who insist that the originals are impossible to match because magnets and wire with the same exact formula and specifications from the past are impossible to find today?

*Yes, I think it is impossible to match modern wire with vintage wire, it is a small difference, but the big picture is made entirely of small pieces.*

*Magnets can be made in much the same way, when I talk to my supplier in the UK, they can do anything I need. They have analyzed many vintage P.A.F.s and Pat. No. magnets and they perform a perfect recreation; not only in sound, but in looks too. The same is true with steel parts; each and every detail can be replicated. When I am winding I always try to replicate that factor of vintage wire detail with my winding.*

Are there details of the originals which are particularly difficult to get right?

*In the beginning everything was difficult, I had to do it all from scratch; from buying real P.A.F.s, unwinding many broken ones for restoration, doing accurate CAD drawings, talking to many tool makers (until I found one local guy who is a genius and can do anything I can imagine), buying half ton heavy vintage winding machine for making perfect recreation of P.A.F. pickups, etc. If I knew in the beginning it would take ten years and a big bag of cash to do it, I would most likely have stuck with the luthier work I was doing. But I just couldn't find the proper pickups for my builds, and it had to be done the right way (of course).*

Is there something in the way the originals were built that you found interesting from a manufacturing point of view? Is there something that surprised or intrigued you?

*Yes, I find everything about them interesting! I just marvel at the design and every single aspect of P.A.F. pickups. The tiny details and minute mistakes that were made when manufacturing the molds for the bobbins and M69 mounting rings are especially interesting for me. Baseplate feet markings, cover shapes and their specific nickel plating process and I even find the buffing patterns interesting. Every single aspect is intriguing and requires delicate attention to detail in order to recreate them these days.*

Do you use fully charged magnets or magnets charged to a given strength to get vintage tones? Is there a certain type of AlNiCo that you prefer to work with?

*I don't use them fully charged, but I get them fully charged and then match them to my favorite P.A.F. pickups in my collection. I love to match them to my '59 double cream P.A.F. pickup. I prefer to work with AlNiCo 4 magnets because they were mostly used in 1959 on the best of the best P.A.F. examples. They are also the easiest to calibrate the neck with the bridge, so that they are a sonic match.*

Do you offer repair/restoration services?

*Yes of course, I offer restoration and repair free of charge. I even pay the shipping to return them to the customer, and I can supply any missing parts for free. I will do anything to learn as much as I can about them!*

# Conclusion

The fifties were an incredible decade in the history of the electric guitar. While not invented in the fifties, it is in those years that the solid body guitar matured and became a globally accepted instrument. Leo Fender, with the Stratocaster, proved that new shapes could be used with no relation to any acoustic version. Also, innovations in hardware improved intonation and functionality (e.g., Gibson's Tune-O-Matic bridge and Fender's integrated bridge/vibrato), and the Gibson ES 300 Series brought unprecedented versatility, marrying the arch-top and solid body concepts. Further, in the electronics department, many new ideas were experimented with, including stereo outputs (e.g., Rickenbacker, Gretsch, and Gibson) and complex controls (e.g., Fender's Jaguar and Jazzmaster).

Not everything was successful, as most players did not like the fancier, more complicated stuff, but undeniably any new shape, wiring configuration, hardware upgrade or even finish, introduced during the ensuing decades, can be seen as simple refinements on something invented in the fifties (or even earlier). Even active circuitry comes from the past, as Orbra Wallace Appleton, a true visionary, invented an active system in 1943, called the "Velocity Pickup" (Patent number US3518353). This system was finally realized in 1968, when transistor miniaturized circuitry allowed it to be inserted it in a guitar (the Appleton '68 guitar), and in the mid-fifties he also made the first ever aluminum neck guitar (the APP 2).

In fact, the P.A.F. pickups designed in the fifties remain the most desired and copied pickups today, and the principles behind the Gibson humbucking pickup are the same as they were then on a wide variety of models; from the miniaturized units made for the Stratocaster to the many overwound variants being offered.

We think that the enduring popularity of the original is due to the delicate balance between tone, sustain, dynamic range and power. Compared to other products of that era, it is also, as were most things produced by Gibson at the time, quite aesthetically appealing. Even if the product in and of itself is quite simple from a technological point of view, that balance is due to the combination of several parameters that only in the last decade have been properly analyzed and understood. From the materials chosen to the type of magnet, the wire, the assembly, the covers... everything contributed to the end result. The slightest change in this self-contained system could result in a subtle (or substantial) loss of transparency or dynamics, while if an attempt were made to get more power the consequences may be a loss of definition, touch sensitivity and/or articulation.

To those who love the original "Patent Applied For" pickup, even their inconsistencies are appealing, giving a unique and individual character to each unit. Nowadays knowledge, technology and talent allow some of the best winders to build replicas which accentuate some of those inconsistencies, and are convincingly close to the originals. Some even go as far as trying to reproduce some of their mojo by using proprietary aging techniques.
To some, nothing quite compares to the originals, while to others, some replicas are good enough

to give them what they want as far as performance and looks are concerned. In the end, the replica market itself is a magnificent tribute to the validity of that design and many players, famous or unknown, are still performing, live and in the studio, with original guitars from that era, and those who cannot afford one, use the best Reissue they can find.
Bearing in mind the historical importance of the "Patent Applied For" pickup, what's striking is its popularity after sixty years, despite all the incredible changes in technology, culture, musical styles and tastes.

Our opinion is that in the fifties and early sixties, the electric guitar reached its evolutionary peak, just as the violin and the piano did in the 18th Century. As with everything human, there is always room for some improvement and refining of small details, but in essence, the electric guitar was defined in those years. While Gibson did not invent the humbucking pickup, the specific application of those principles, as conceived by Seth Lover, proved to be the most effective, not only for contemporary music styles, but for those of the future as well.

Sure, there was the Gretsch Filter'Tron, but as beautiful as its voice can be, it lacked the power engine needed. Even if in the seventies a plethora of high output pickups were designed, when extra gain became available from the amps, and a vast array of overdrive pedals hit the market, players rediscovered the versatility and airy tones of the original Gibson humbucking pickup.

The golden era of the electric guitar brought many excellent models, from the P 90 to the Dyna-Sonic, from the Filter'Tron to the shiny Fender models. Nonetheless, the Gibson "Patent Applied For" Pickup and its finest replicas remain hard to beat for their ability to cover the broadest range of musical styles. In the right hands and on the right guitar with an appropriate rig the undeniable result can sometimes be pure magic.

PATENT
APPLIED FOR

# Photo Credits

Photografic Tours **"1941 Gibson Lap steel"** on page 39, **"1957 Pre-Decal-P.A.F."** on page 63, **"1959 P.A.F. from a Gibson ES 345TD"** on page 77, **"1959 P.A.F."** on page 87, **"1960's Pre-T-Top P.A.F. Bobbin Patent Number Decal Pickup Repair"** on page 98 and **"1960's Patent Decal T-Top"** on page 103, all text and photos, courtesy of James Finnerty. **"DeArmond pickup"** on page 44, P.A.F. pickups on pages 67, 69, 76, 79. **"Assorted bar magnets"** on page 82, all photos on page 85, page 110 bottom, page 115, **"DiMarzio Super Distortion"** on page 120, courtesy of ***James Finnerty.***

Pier Paolo Adda and Ted McCarty on page 30, courtesy of ***Pier Paolo Adda.***

Photos on pages 22 Heritage H535, courtesy of ***Danilo Alessandro;*** Gibson 79RVT, page 126 photos top, bottom left, courtesy of ***Pepita Pardo.***

Photos on pages 56 (bottom left) and 95 (top left), courtesy of ***Jeffrey Allen.***

Photo on page 47 (top left), courtesy of ***Alex Angelucci.***

Photos on pages 48 and 49, courtesy of ***Jamie Appleton and Carl Grefenstette (owappleton.com).***

Photos on pages 57 and 95 (centre right), courtesy of ***Vincenzo Atzori.***

Photos on pages 6, 19, 22 (bottom left), 29, 31, 51, courtesy of ***Francesco Balossino.***

Photos on pages 15 (top right), 43 (bottom left), 44 (bottom right), 107 (bottom right), 119 (circle), 121 (bottom right), courtesy of ***Claudio Caldana.***

"Les Paul and Mary Ford", on page 36, courtesy of ***Centerstream Publishing.***

Photos on pages 7, 107 (bottom left-centre), courtesy of ***Fabrizio Dadò.***

Photos on page 126 (top and right), courtesy of ***Duane Flowers.***

Photos on pages 8, 20 (top), 95 (top right and bottom left), 102, courtesy of ***Stefano Gaibazzi (Re Caster).***

Photo on page 33, courtesy of ***Cole Gaskins.***

Photo on page 50, courtesy of the ***Fred Gretsch Enterprises.***

"Zebra P.A.F." on page 69 and photos on pages 72 and 73, courtesy of ***Jon Gundry.***

Gibson Factory photos on pages 10 and 16, by Mamie L. Austin and Ted McCarty's photo on page 17, courtesy of the ***Kalamazoo Valley Museum of Kalamazoo, Michigan***

Vintage Les Paul Models, on pages 3, 109, 116, 130 and 140, courtesy of ***Kunio Kishido.***

"1956 Les Paul Custom" on pages 44 and 45, courtesy of ***John Kontos.***

Photos on pages 11, 14, 38 (circle) and 42, courtesy of ***Lowell Levinger (Players Vintage Instruments).***

Photos on pages 12 and 13, by Mamie L. Austin, courtesy of the ***Kalamazoo Public Library in Kalamazoo, Michigan.***

Photo on page 15, "Gibson GA 40T", courtesy of ***Eva Passerini.***

Photos on pages 22 (circle), 24, 56 (bottom right), 58, 69 (centre right), 95 (centre left), 113, courtesy of ***Furio Pozzi.***

Photos on pages 9, 46, 53, 55, 59, 118, 119, 121 (bottom left), by Alex Solca, courtesy of ***Axe Guitar Magazine, Edizioni Palomino.***

Photos on pages 36 (bottom right) and 47 (top right), courtesy of ***Dave Stephens.***

Photos on pages 1, 3 (bottom), 8 (bottom right), 15 (bottom left), 20 (bottom), 43 (bottom right, top left), 47 (bottom, left and right), 55 (center), 60, 62, 68, 69 (top), 71, 75, 82 (bottom), 92, 93, 106, 110 top, 126 (bottom right-centre), 168, 169 courtesy of ***Aleksandar Vrhovec.***

Photos on pages 32, 34, 38, courtesy of ***Lynn Weelwright.***

# Bibliography


**The Story Of Paul A. Bigsby: The Father Of The Modern Electric Solidbody Guitar**
*By Andy Babiuk - FG Publishing (2009)*

**Million Dollar Les Paul: In search of the most valuable guitar in the world**
*By Tony Bacon - Jawbone Press (2008)*

**SUNBURST: HOW THE GIBSON LES PAUL STANDARD BECAME A LEGENDARY GUITAR**
*By Tony Bacon - Backbeat UK (2014)*

**The SG Guitar Book: 50 Years of Gibson's Stylish Solid Guitar**
*By Tony Bacon- Backbeat Books (2015)*

**Gibson Guitars: 100 Years of an American Icon**
*By Walter Carter - General Publishing Group (1994)*

**The Gibson 'Burst: 1958-1960**
*By Jay Scott, Vic DaPra - Centerstream Publishing (2007)*

**Burst Believers I, II, and III**
*By Vic DaPra - Centerstream (2016)*

**Gibson Electrics - The Classic Years**
*By A. R. Duchossoir - Hal Leonard (1998)*

**Gibson Electric Steel Guitars: 1935-1967**
*By A. R. Duchossoir - Hal Leonard (2009)*

**Gibson Guitars: Ted McCarty's Golden Era: 1948-1966**
*By Gil Hembree - GH Books (2007)*

**The Gibson Les Paul: The Illustrated History of the Guitar That Changed Rock**
*By Dave Hunter - Voyager Press (2017)*

**The Gibson 335: Its History and Its Players**
*By Adrian Ingram - Centerstream Publishing (2006)*

**BEAUTY OF THE BURST**
*By Yasuhido Iwanade - Hal Leonard (1999)*

**The Early Years of the Les Paul Legacy 1915-1963**
*By Robb Lawrence - Hal Leonard (2008)*

**The Modern Era of the Les Paul Legacy: 1968-2009**
*By Robb Lawrence - Hal Leonard (2009)*

**Gibson Amplifiers 1933-2008: 75 Years of the Gold Tone**
*By Wallace Marx, Jr - Alfred Music (2009)*

# Index

# More Great Books from Centerstream...